THE GOLDEN ELIXIR
OF THE WEST

THE GOLDEN ELIXIR
OF THE WEST

Whiskey and the Shaping of America

SHERRY MONAHAN
WITH JANE PERKINS

Preface by David Perkins

TWODOT®

GUILFORD. CONNECTICUT
HELENA, MONTANA

A · TWODOT® · BOOK

An imprint of Globe Pequot
A registered trademark of Rowman & Littlefield

Distributed by NATIONAL BOOK NETWORK

British Library Cataloguing in Publication Information available

Library of Congress Cataloging-in-Publication Data available

ISBN 978-1-4930-2849-8 (hardcover)
ISBN 978-1-4930-2850-4 (e-book)

♾™ The paper used in this publication meets the minimum requirements of American National Standard for Information Sciences—Permanence of Paper for Printed Library Materials, ANSI/NISO Z39.48-1992.

Printed in the United States of America

Contents

Preface

In the early days of starting High West Whiskey, Jane and I were regularly asked, "Why are you starting a whiskey distillery . . . and in Utah of all places?" People were curious about why we decided to uproot a great life in the San Francisco Bay area, move to Utah, and take a chance doing something that no one had done *legally* since 1870. We initially answered peoples' questions by showing them historical photographs of saloons in Utah and asking them two questions, "What are these people drinking and where are they drinking?"

Everyone responded to the first part of the question with one quick word: "whiskey." Most responded to the second part of the question with, "Saloons, and they are . . . somewhere out west." Amazingly all the photographs came from the Utah Historical Society. Although Utah is known by most people for its non-drinking pioneers, namely the pious Mormons, the fact is that Utah was also, in the early days, filled with whiskey-making, whiskey-drinking miners, pioneers, and cowboys who were simply following in the footsteps of other westerners. Consider the following quote:

> *Brigham Young and the priesthood manufactured a most villainous brand of whiskey known as Valley Tan, and dispensed it to the Saints at high figures.*
> —Emmeline B. Wells, editor,
> *Woman's Exponent*, 1879

The stories of whiskey and its involvement in the formation of the American West are heavily embedded with nostalgia, humor, tragedy, and success. The big question for us then became, "If the West's formation and history is so inextricably tied to whiskey, why aren't there any whiskey distilleries here today in the twenty-first century, or at least more western brands of whiskey?"

This became our inspiration for founding a distillery in Park City, Utah, naming our new whiskey "High West," and attempting to carry on the traditions that were a way of life in the early days of the state. This book is a vehicle for us to uncover the facts behind all the stories, lore, and legends, to find out how much was true, and then to fully understand whiskey's role in the West. How did whiskey get west in the first place? Why whiskey and not some other spirit? Who really drank whiskey? How much did they really drink? What did they drink with it? Did cowboys drink on the trail? Did people other than gunslingers and saloon patrons drink whiskey as well? How did whiskey affect the growth of the American West?

These are but a few of the questions we will attempt to answer and is what inspired us to become involved with this project.

—DAVID PERKINS, JANUARY 2017

I was inspired to become involved with this book because of my love for the American West. I also love to share the untold stories and little-known facts about the pioneers and daily life with my readers. Most people associate whiskey with the West, but few know how pivotal whiskey really was in shaping it. It was used as a tool to barter with, treat wounds, blow off some steam at the end of a cattle trail, and drown sorrows. Whiskey employed many pioneers, from explorers to trappers and distillers to saloonkeepers and more. It drove the transportation industry and aided in the creation of taxes and regulations. By writing this book, I hope readers will walk away with a new appreciation of the golden elixir and the role it had in a history that only Americans can claim—the Wild West.

—SHERRY MONAHAN

Introduction

A COWBOY SAUNTERS INTO A SALOON WITH SWINGING DOORS slapping behind him and walks up to ask the bartender for a straight shot of whiskey—in western movies and books, it's a scene that is practically compulsory. Why it's largely not accurate is another story, but there's no denying that whiskey and the West have forever been linked in western history. Whiskey was the golden elixir of the West and king of the distilled spirits. It was an integral part of the great western expansion and has strong ties to early explorers, pioneers, the railroads, and the cattle era. It was sold as medicine, used to barter with, and often gave courage where there was none. Whiskey's role in shaping the West, and its rise to prominence over rum or vodka, has its roots in the early days of the United States. It's a story of taxes, availability, and profits.

Because corn, wheat, barley, and rye—the main ingredients in whiskey—were easily grown all over North America, the art of distilling spread as rapidly as settlers into newly settled regions. Whiskey was quick and easy to produce. And distilling grains into alcohol made them more valuable, more transportable, and more easily stored for long periods. As whiskey's popularity increased, so did its value as a trade good.

Early explorers Meriwether Lewis, William Clark, and Zebulon Pike took whiskey along with them on their expeditions. In addition to its being a standard army ration, it was used as a reward for their men and for trading purposes. Later, trappers like Jim Bridger, Kit Carson, and Jedediah Smith carried it with them as a trade good—and soon after the practice started, they all quickly learned that the native peoples wouldn't trade with them if they didn't include whiskey in the bargaining process.

As whiskey became more profitable as a commodity during the fur trading era, producers had a hard time keeping up with the demand. Businessmen who wanted to turn a quick profit and fill their coffers created "rectified" whiskey products that were watered down or doctored with other cheaper ingredients like tobacco juice, kerosene, or grain alcohol. Straight whiskey was aged in new oak barrels for a minimum of two years, whereas rectified whiskey was usually consumed immediately, requiring no aging, and was often further distilled. Many whiskey peddlers and saloon owners made their own version of whiskey. Elixirs and bitters were also available and were another common way that both men and women pioneers could get drunk.

With its value as a trade commodity firmly established in the West, it was only natural that as the frontier expanded so did

Whiskey peddlers were prominent in western towns. They traveled the West setting up medicine shows to demonstrate their cure-alls. Dakota Territory, circa 1900s. NATIONAL ARCHIVES

whiskey-based entrepreneurship. Pioneers opened a variety of whiskey-related businesses, and a host of other enterprises were formed in the West to support its swelling population. Businesses like stagecoaches, freighters, glass and bottle companies, barrel makers, distributors, hotels, railroads, cities, gamblers, distillers, mining, salesmen, and saloons all thrived because of whiskey.

Businesses all across the West boomed with whiskey, but none more than the saloons, dance halls, and brothels. Other than the distillers themselves, the men and women involved with these businesses undoubtedly had the biggest connection to, and profited the most from, whiskey's influence. They were the epicenter of most towns, the place where men gathered to get their news, talk politics, and unwind, thereby further establishing whiskey's influence in the shaping of the West. In money towns like Tombstone, Arizona; Virginia City, Nevada; or Dodge City, Kansas, popular whiskey drinks of the day included Whiskey Cocktails, Whiskey Slings, Whiskey Punches, Rock and Rye, and Stone Fences. More often than not, saloon owners in rural or poorer towns would serve their customers a simple shot of rotgut or cheap whiskey in plain buildings that offered little save a basic bar and a few glasses.

The Golden Elixir of the West follows whiskey's influence in five main movements that helped make up the settlement of the West: early trailblazing, adventurous pioneers, mining, the cattle era, and the railroad. The stories of the pioneers themselves illuminate how whiskey became an integral part of the expanding American West.

Firsthand stories from those who were there, facts about whiskey, including how it was made and distributed, and the social mores of a whiskey-drinking population bolster and debunk some of the myths of the West. Also included are period photos and recipes for historical cocktails made with whiskey.

Please note that we have not corrected grammar in quoted texts so the reader can gain a full understanding of the content as it was written. In this book, you will see whiskey spelled "whiskey" and "whisky" in quoted text. The word was commonly spelled both ways during the nineteenth century, and it depended upon the writer as to which spelling was used.

Mark Twain summed up just how much whiskey and the West are tied together in his book *Life on the Mississippi*. He penned, "How solemn and beautiful is the thought, that the earliest pioneer of civilization, the van-leader of civilization, is never the steamboat, never the railroad, never the newspaper, never the Sabbath-school, never the missionary—but always whiskey!"

Grab a glass of your favorite whiskey or whip up a cocktail and enjoy!

CHAPTER ONE

Early Trailblazing:
Explorers and Traders

On a sunny June 29, 1804, at their camp at the mouth of the Kansas River, Captains Meriwether Lewis and William Clark convened an outdoor court-martial. Just a month into the legendary expedition of the Corps of Discovery, they were forced to take disciplinary action because some of the men had abused their whiskey supply. Privates John Collins and Hugh Hall were charged with being drunk and with providing the drink, respectively. Captain Clark wrote, "A Court martial will Set this day at 11 oClock, to Consist of five members, for the trial of John Collins and Hugh Hall, Confined on Charges exhibited against them by Sergeant Floyd, agreeable to the articles of War."

Collins was formally charged with and found guilty of "getting drunk on his post this morning out of whiskey put under his Charge as a Sentinel and for Suffering Hugh Hall to draw whiskey out of the Said Barrel intended for the party." As the man in charge of guarding the whiskey, Collins was sentenced to 100 lashes on his bare back. Hugh Hall pleaded guilty to taking whiskey he had no right to, was found guilty, and was sentenced to 50 lashes on his bare back. Their sentences were immediately carried out, and at four that afternoon, Collins and Hall with their

Soldier in barrel is labeled "Too fond of whiskey; forged an order on the surgeon," with one soldier saying to him, "How are you Monitor?" and another saying, "Where's the Merrimac?" Circa 1862. LIBRARY OF CONGRESS

battered backs, along with the rest of the expedition, packed up and continued on their journey.[1]

President Thomas Jefferson's 1803 purchase of the Louisiana Territory from France—some 900,000 square miles of North American land—was the first step in the settling of the great American West by the former citizens of Britain who had recently gained their independence. Before the purchase only a handful of settlements existed in the French-ruled area. In 1800 New Orleans was the largest "western" city, with some eight thousand inhabitants. A small town called Cincinnati had been established in the middle of what was then known as the Northwest Territory, and Spanish missions dotted the Southwest and California. To Americans, the newly acquired Louisiana Territory was a vast, unknown, and unexplored space. Most easterners had no idea what the landscape looked like, if anyone lived there, or how long it would take to reach the Pacific Ocean. That didn't stop the speculation, and the possibilities for the vast land filled the minds of the men and women of the newly formed nation where just about anything could happen. Farmers dreamed of land for crops, and businessmen dreamed of creating empires from natural resources. And there was a great hope that a clear and easy route might be found to assist in trade between the newly created United States of America and the Far East. After the purchase of the territory, Jefferson wrote, "The geography of the Missouri and the most convenient water communication to the Pacific Ocean is a desideratum not yet satisfied."[2]

Jefferson's curiosity was as strong as his hope of a straightforward northwest passage, and he moved quickly to satisfy his desire to gain knowledge about the new territory. He immediately laid plans for its exploration by assembling a capable and daring team to make their way across America's vast new acquisition.

Jefferson tapped his personal secretary, Meriwether Lewis, who in turn recruited his former army friend, William Clark, to lead an expedition to the Pacific Ocean over the northern portion of the Louisiana Territory. Those two intrepid men would lead what became known as the Corps of Discovery to explore and document new sights, plot rivers, meet the indigenous people, and collect information about the flora and fauna as well as specimens to send home to Virginia when they could. Jefferson wrote to Lewis on June 20, 1803, "The object of your mission is to explore the Missouri river, & such principal stream of it, as, by its course & communication with the waters of the Pacific Ocean, may offer the most direct & practicable water communication across this continent, for the purposes of commerce."[3]

By the time Lewis and Clark had assembled their trade goods and supplies for the journey west, the native peoples along their planned route had already become accustomed to the use of whiskey as a trade good and—in fact—demanded it. French traders had established the whiskey negotiation as part of their regular commerce with the natives they encountered. Major

Thomas Biddle, who would be on the later Yellowstone Expedition up the Missouri, wrote, "So violent is the attachment of the Indian for it [liquor] that he who gives most is sure to obtain furs, while should anyone attempt to trade without it he is sure of losing ground with this antagonist. No bargain is ever made without it."[4]

Lewis and Clark were aware of this trading expectation, and so whiskey was included in their detailed planning for rations, equipment, and trade goods for their expedition. Whiskey was also a standard United States Army ration and was used as a reward for good behavior and for medical purposes. In August 1803 when Meriwether Lewis prepared a preliminary list of items to be taken on the journey, under the category of "Provisions and Subsistence," he added spices, portable soup, rock salt, and "6 Kegs of 5 Gallons each making 30 Gallons of rectified spirits such as is used for the Indian trade." (Rectified spirits were distilled spirits, redistilled or reprocessed to remove contaminants and then enhanced with various flavorings.)[5]

A few months later, despite the cold, the expedition began building Camp Dubois on the banks of the River Dubois near the mouth of the Missouri in December 1803. The location, in what is now Illinois, was selected to serve as a military camp and their staging ground as the men prepared for their journey to commence the following year. The men, while waiting to depart, performed regular duties, participated in drills, and grew both anxious and bored. Despite watching supplies arriving and boats being readied, the men grew restless as winter dragged on and ice ran in the river and in their veins.

Their first Christmas together at the camp was cold and snowy. They were also far from everything and just about everyone they knew, alone save some local Indians, squatters, a few traders in the area, and other passersby. Clark knew his men were anxious to begin navigating uncharted waters, so after their turkey dinner when they drank too much whiskey, he showed tolerance. He knew it might be the last merry-making they would do for quite some time. He wrote in his journal, "I was wakened by a Christmas discharge found that some of the party had got drunk (2 fought), the men frolicked and hunted all day, Snow this morning, Ice run all day, Several Turkey Killed. Shields returned with a cheese & 4 lb. butter, Three Indians Come to day to take Christmas with us, I gave them a bottle of whiskey and they went off after informing me that a great talk had been held and that all the nations were going to war against the Ozous [Osage?] in 3 months."[6]

In February 1804 Lewis and Clark added 593 rations of whiskey to the expedition's stores as a reward for work done so far and as an incentive for the crew of thirty. Lewis issued detachment orders that stated "men who are engaged in making sugar [and other jobs] will continue in that employment until further orders, and will receive each a half a gill of extra whiskey per day and be exempt from guard duty. . . . No whiskey shall in future be delivered from the Contractor's store except for the legal ration, and as appropriated by this order, unless otherwise directed by Captain Clark or myself."[7] He did the same thing for good behavior on April 13, when "at 10 oClock I arrived in Majr. Rumseys boat from St Louis, with Sundery articles for our voyage, a Cloudy day. I hoist a Flag Staff, After part of the day fair, river falling. I give out to the men Lead, Powder, & an extra gill of Whiskey—5$ of Cap Lew at St Louis."[8]

Despite Lewis's generous "good behavior whiskey," four of their men, Wiser, Robinson, Coulter, and Boyle, left the camp to get drunk. They sneaked out under false pretenses to frequent a neighboring whiskey shop. Lewis advised Sergeant Ordway to read the men's names on the parade ground and to punish them publicly with the hope that others would not be so reckless. Lewis sentenced them to ten days' confinement at the camp. He wrote in his notes, "The Commanding officer feels himself mortifyed and disappointed at the disorderly conduct of Reubin Fields, in refusing to mount guard when in the due roteen [routine] of duty

Whiskey played a vital role in the US Army and on government expeditions. While Lewis served Washington during the Whiskey Rebellion and later during the Corps of Discovery expedition from 1804–1806, whiskey was given as rations of a "gill cup." Lewis wrote about the abundance of whiskey in this letter to his mother. Note the last sentence: "We have mountains of beef and sums of whiskey and I feel myself able to share it."

MISSOURI STATE HISTORY MUSEUM

he was regularly warned. . . . The abuse of some of the party with respect to the prevelege heretofore granted them of going into the country, is not less displeasing; to such as have made hunting or other business a pretext to cover their design of visiting a neighbouring whiskey shop, he cannot for the present extend this prevelige; and dose therefore most positively direct, that Colter, Bolye, Wiser, and Robinson do not recieve permission to leave camp under any pretext whatever for ten days." Lewis's anger no doubt stemmed from the fact that if the men couldn't follow orders at a camp in a civilized location, how would they react when in the wilds on the frontier. He was right to worry, and the penalties for insubordination and drunkenness grew harsher over time.[9]

Despite the occasional drunkenness that resulted in swift punishment, whiskey served as a commodity and morale booster, and was used to "warm the body and soul" on many occasions as the expedition continued west. Nearly a year after the Corps' Christmas revelry at Camp Dubois, on a snowy November 13, 1804, Captain Lewis went out exploring and Sergeant Ordway was left in charge, as was protocol. Ordway was not as generous in giving the expedition's whiskey to natives as his commander had been earlier. He recorded notes of his encounter with some Lakota (Sioux) and Mandan: "Snowey morning. the Ice run considerable fast in the river. . . . Capt. Lewis & 6 men went in the pearogue [pirogue] up the River through the Ice to the first village of the Mandens [Mandans] after Stone for the backs of our Chimneys. Some of the Sioux Indians [6] came here with a chief of the Mandens. They asked for whiskey &.C. [etc.] but we Gave them none. Capt. Lewis returned with his party towards evening much fatigued. They got fast on a Sand bar & had to be out in the water abto. [about] 2 hours. The Ice running against their legs. Their close frooze on them. one of them got 1 of his feet frost bit. It hapned that they had Some whiskey with them to revive their Spirits."[10]

Eight months later, after grueling, backbreaking labor, traversing unknown waterways and meeting new inhabitants, the expedition celebrated the birth of America in 1805 at the Great Falls, in what is now Montana. Much to their frustration, they had been stuck in the area for over a month trying to navigate the river's treacherous drop. Their mood was greatly improved after the captains issued whiskey to all the men in honor of Independence Day. It was the last of their supply for some time to come. After their stomachs were satisfied with a meal of beans and bacon, suet dumplings, and buffalo meat, some of the men drew their fiddles to play while others danced to the music that filled the summer air. Lewis wrote, "We gave the men a drink of Sperits, it being the last of our stock, and some of them appeared a little sensible of its effects. . . . In short we had no just cause to covet the sumptuous feasts of our countrymen on this day" Sergeant Ordway also noted the occasion: "It being the 4th of Independence we drank the last of our ardent spirits except a little reserved for sickness."[11]

The trip around the Great Falls foreshadowed further hardship to come as the men continued their march west over mountains packed with snow and then finally reached the Pacific Ocean. With minimal supplies in March 1806, the flea-bitten crew, longing for home, made their way back East after spending a winter on the coast. They hadn't tasted whiskey since July at the Great Falls the previous year. The heat of summer brought out mosquitoes that swarmed them on the Missouri River as they neared their destination. None of them could have been happier than Captain Clark when they met a trading boat and acquired a gallon of whiskey in early September. Clark promptly issued a dram to each man. On September 14, as they entered the portion of the river in Kansas, to Clark's further delight, they encountered three young men named Lacroy, Aiten, and Coutau [Choteau?] from St. Louis. He wrote, "Those young men received us with great friendship and pressed on us some whisky for our men, bisquet, pork and onions, & part of their Stores."

Good fortune continued for this tired and itchy crew as they traversed two treacherous miles of the swift-moving river. A couple of days later they were gleefully met by a Captain McClellan, who had heard—as it was generally assumed by many—that their entire expedition had been killed. They traded McClellan a barrel of corn for some much welcomed supplies that included chocolate, sugar, biscuits, and "as much whiskey as they would drink."[12]

Without whiskey for morale and trade, the Corps of Discovery's expedition might have been quite different. Still, despite not plotting a clear and easy northwest water route for the American fur trading business, Lewis and Clark had successfully reached the Pacific Ocean and returned home to tell about it. Their reports and glorious tales caused curious excitement about the vast and open frontier. A man named Thomas James recalled the return of the expedition and the effect it had on him and other Americans: "In the fall of this year, Lewis and Clark returned from Oregon and the Pacific Ocean, whither they had been sent by the administration of Jefferson in the first exploring expedition west of the Rocky Mountains, and their accounts of that wild region, with those of their companions, first excited a spirit of trafficking adventure among the young men of the West."

While Lewis and Clark were attempting to plot the much sought after Northwest Passage, Lieutenant Zebulon Pike departed St. Louis in August 1805 to make his way up the Mississippi River and then to explore lands to the south and west of the Corps of Discovery's intended path. General James Wilkinson, who was the military governor of the Louisiana Territory, had directed Pike to map the lands and convince the resident Indians to let Americans build forts on their land. Pike would barter for those rights with liquor, but instead of giving the Indians straight whiskey, Pike offered them "made whiskey," which was whiskey cut in half with water. It kept them sober longer and extended his supply, and helped Pike establish solid relations in the region. After the success of his first effort, Pike was sent on another mission to

Zebulon Pike's father, Captain Zebulon Montgomery Pike, who served during Washington's time, ordered whiskey for his men for good behavior. This 1794 letter entitles the bearer to "one quart of whisky for having made the first part of the way." NEW YORK PUBLIC LIBRARY DIGITAL COLLECTIONS

explore the area now known as Arkansas and then to continue into other areas of the Southwest. During his journey, he ascended the Grand Peak, in what is now Colorado, on November 27, 1806. By 1843 it was called Pike's Peak.[13]

In the years following Lewis and Clark's and Pike's expeditions, trade routes opened up, the fur trade exploded, and businessmen like Spaniard Manuel Lisa, German-American John Jacob Astor, and General William Ashley established profitable businesses along the trade routes that grew from those explorations. Ashley employed such well-known men as Jim Bridger, Jedediah Smith, James Beckwourth, and Thomas James as scouts, trappers, and traders. They began their trapping and trading journeys armed with kegs or casks of whiskey for business and personal use, and they began to mark additional routes and to establish trading posts and forts.

Thomas James, a native of Illinois who worked for Manuel Lisa, recalled his time with Lisa's Missouri Fur Company: "The Missouri Fur Company had just been formed, and they projected an expedition up the Missouri and to the Rocky Mountains, which was to start in the spring of the following year, 1809. . . . In five days after entering the Missouri, we descended to the Gros

Ventre village and our Fort, and were there joyfully received by our old companions. Whiskey flowed like milk and honey in the land of Canaan, being sold to the men by the disinterested and benevolent gentlemen of the Missouri Fur Company, for the moderate sum of twelve dollars per gallon, they taking in payment, beaver skins at one dollar and a half, each, which were worth in St. Louis, six. Their prices for everything else were in about the same proportion. Even at this price some of the men bought whiskey by the bucket full, and drank 'Till they forgot their loves and debts And cared for grief na mair.'" Lewis and Clark had outfitted their team with whiskey at $1.28 per gallon five years earlier. Because whiskey was in such high demand by both the men at the trading post and the Indians, the price of whiskey was marked up by about 600 percent at this newly built trading post.[14]

As trade increased and the population of traders burgeoned, William Ashley saw a need and an opportunity that would benefit his business. In the spring of 1825, he founded the first rendezvous in the Rocky Mountains, which would become an annual gathering that afforded the local Indians and mountain men the opportunity to trade the previous year's pelts and refit themselves for the next trapping season at one time in one location. As trappers, traders, Indians, and others arrived at the rendezvous site, they set up their tepees and tents around the grounds of the post, and a makeshift camp appeared. Rendezvous posts were usually protected by fences or stockade walls surrounding the buildings that housed business, sleeping, and dining quarters. The rendezvous was a time of great excitement, and smells from campfires wafted into the air while attendees bargained, laughed, danced, and drank freely. Not everyone camped in the same area, and some traders were miles apart from one another. They all had the same goal—selling and buying at the best price.

When Ashley created his provisions list for the rendezvous, whiskey was *not* one of the items on it. However, his man Beckwourth, who was with the group, had some at the event. He recalled, "On arriving at the rendezvous, we found the main body of the Salt Lake party already there with the whole of their effects. The general would open none of his goods, except tobacco, until all had arrived, as he wished to make an equal distribution; for goods were then very scarce in the mountains, and hard to obtain. When all had come in, he opened his goods, and there was a general jubilee among all at the rendezvous. We constituted quite a little town, numbering at least eight hundred souls, of whom one half were women and children. There were some among us who had not seen any groceries, such as coffee, sugar, &c., for several months. The whisky went off as freely as water, even at the exorbitant price he sold it for. All kinds of sports were indulged in with a heartiness that would astonish more civilized societies. The general transacted a very profitable trade with our Salt Lake friends." Knowing whiskey was vital to the rendezvous, the list of provisions thereafter always included a good supply.

Beckwourth later recalled another rendezvous: "The absent parties began to arrive, one after the other, at the rendezvous. Shortly after, General Ashley and Mr. Sublet [Sublette] came in, accompanied with three hundred pack mules, well laden with goods and all things necessary for the mountaineers and the Indian trade. It may well be supposed that the arrival of such a vast amount of luxuries from the East did not pass off without a general celebration. Mirth, songs, dancing, shouting, trading, running, jumping, singing, racing, target-shooting, yarns, frolic, with all sorts of extravagances that white men or Indians could invent, were freely indulged in. The unpacking of the medicine water contributed not a little to the heightening of our festivities."

Whiskey was continuing to exert a powerful influence on trade in the West and was important to business at every rendezvous and part and parcel of the business of trading. The popularity of fashionable beaver hats in the East and in Europe ensured that the rendezvous would last for fifteen years, until silk became the latest fashion trend for hats and the poor beaver had been nearly

Rendezvous camp at Cheyenne, Wyoming, 1871. Rendezvous gatherings took place in the Rocky Mountains and were an opportunity for trappers and traders to exchange their pelts as well as buy whiskey and wares and commune with fellow mountain men. NATIONAL ARCHIVES

hunted to extinction.[15] Even as the fur trade dwindled due to the depletion of resources and the change of fashion, however, the whiskey trade was becoming an economic force that supplemented the fur trade business. Eventually, whiskey turned out to be the better commodity.

Pioneers had been heading to Oregon as early as the 1830s, and as immigration to the West exploded during the mid-nineteenth century, the days of rough mountain men living in near solitude or coexisting peacefully among the natives was coming to an end. Families were increasingly establishing settlements and changing the native inhabitants' way of life, though single men still made up the vast majority of residents on the frontier and the West was still seen to be a wild, uncouth place. In the southwest, some excited emigrants headed to Texas to claim free land from the Mexican government. The only requirement was that they swear an allegiance to Mexico. By 1836 some thirty thousand Americans had moved to Texas. Whiskey, of course, went along for the journey, and some in Texas saw the negative side of inebriation. In 1840 the vice president of Texas, David Burnet, published a book titled *Texas in 1840, or The Emigrant's Guide to the New Republic*. In it he noted that some of the pioneers' habits regarding manners and society were deplorable. He penned, "Justice demands that before closing our remarks upon the society and manners of Texas, we should acknowledge that there are several things to deplore. One of these is a very prevalent habit of profane swearing. This low and senseless vice which has not the form of an excuse, being entirely without temptation, is practised by high and low, senators and judges, officers and citizens. . . . Another very prevailing practice is the drinking of ardent spirits. As yet temperance societies have made but comparatively little progress in this republic. Several have been established, and are shedding around them a happy influence. Still the work is but begun. The friends of temperance, it is presumed, will not pause in their course till the monster's power is curbed and his deadly influence broken. Gambling in one or two places, is said to be in fearful progress. Finally, one of the surest guarantees for success to the emigrant, of whatever business or circumstances, is the entire banishment of ardent spirits from his house and premises. Where these are an allowed guest, no security can be sure to prevent their producing disaster to the man or some part of his household. Entire abstinence alone gives certainty that the insidious poison will never infect one of the favored circle where it is practised."[16]

Over the next decade, as tensions grew between the United States and Mexico over territory and boundaries, the push for the United States to occupy North America increased. Lieutenant John C. Frémont of the Army Topographical Engineers led an expedition into the Rocky Mountains in June 1842 with the object of finding a safe route for emigrants to take to the Oregon

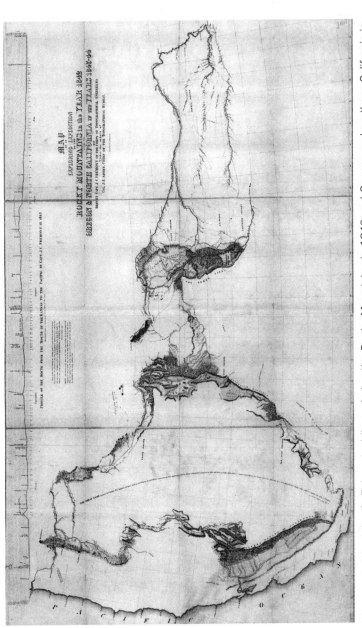

Map created by John C. Frémont while exploring the Rocky Mountains in 1842 and Oregon and northern California in 1843–1844. LIBRARY OF CONGRESS

Territory, where the United States and Britain had agreed to equal trade and settlement rights. Frémont was successful in his quest and returned to St. Louis in October with maps that provided a clear route for the many settlers who were ready to reach the great Pacific. Migration began along the route that would be known as the Oregon Trail. The perceived opportunity to be found in the new country to the west grew.

In 1843, Jim Bridger and Louis Vasquez opened an emigrant trading post along the Oregon Trail in Wyoming called Fort Bridger. The fort saw about one thousand hopeful souls pass through during what would become known as the Great Migration in the first year of the route's existence. Those journeys marked the beginning of the greatest migration in American history. By 1846 the United States had taken ownership of the Oregon Territory from England and was ready to turn its attention to acquiring the territory of Texas, New Mexico, and California, which were owned by Mexico.

In May 1846 the conflict known as the Mexican-American War began, and two years later the Treaty of Hidalgo Guadalupe was signed. Texas, New Mexico, and California were purchased from Mexico and annexed to the United States. Several years later, in 1853, the Gadsden Purchase added additional land between Texas and California. The United States officially stretched from the Atlantic to the Pacific Coast—from "sea to shining sea." The western landscape would soon be forever changed with a little help from a golden elixir called whiskey.

As a flood of emigrants rolled their wagons, handcarts, and livestock across the West, the lives of the peoples who already called the West home would never be the same. Whiskey's popularity as a trade good made it an essential tool in opening up new territory, but its influence compounded the damage that was emigration's legacy for native peoples.

Traders frequently used the Indians' desire for whiskey against them, and whiskey played a major role in dividing and crippling

Pioneers traveled in groups called emigrant trains. Conestoga wagons were referred to as "prairie schooners" because the white canvas reminded them of sailing ships. The Oregon and Mormon Trails were most popular. This image shows pioneers with barrels on the back of their wagons on the Mormon Trail. UTAH STATE HISTORICAL SOCIETY

the natives of the West. Traders served watered-down or rectified products to get the Indians drunk enough to give away all their pelts for next to nothing, but not inebriated to the point of belligerence. Over time the Indians began to understand the traders' tactics, but their dependence on what some called "medicine-water" gave them little room for further negotiation. As alcohol disrupted the communal and spiritual ways of the native peoples, hostilities between the natives and whites increased. But where there was a profit to be made, scruples were ignored.

Entrepreneurs in the West saw a market for whiskey and didn't care about the harm it was causing. In 1833 whiskey was trading at $5 per pint or $40 per gallon—the cost for whiskey in New York was between $29 and $36 per gallon. (In today's money

$40 would be about $990.) Supply and demand was the rule, and whiskey was in great demand.[17]

In 1834 Congress passed the Indian Trade and Intercourse Act, which outlawed the sale of alcohol to Indians. Section 20 of the act read, "And be it further enacted, That if any person shall sell, exchange, give, barter or dispose of, any spirituous liquor or wine to an Indian, (in the Indian country), such person shall forfeit and pay the sum of five hundred dollars; and if any person shall introduce, or attempt to introduce, any spirituous liquor or wine into the Indian country, except such supplies as shall be necessary for the officers of the United States and troops of the service, under the direction of the War Department; such person shall forfeit and pay a sum not exceeding three hundred dollars; and if any superintendent of Indian affairs, Indian agent, sub-agent or commanding officer of a military post, has reason to suspect, or is informed that any white person or Indian is about to introduce or has introduced any spirituous liquor or wine into the Indian country, in violation of the provisions of this section, it shall be lawful for such superintendent, Indian agent or sub-agent, or military officer, agreeably to such regulations as may be established by the President of the United States, to cause the boats, stores, packages, or places of deposit of such persons to be searched, and if any such spirituous liquor or wine is found, the goods, boats, packages, and peltries of such person shall be seized and delivered to the proper officer, and shall be proceeded against by libel in the proper court, and forfeited, one-half to the use of the informer, and the other half to the use of the United States; and if such person is a trader his license shall be revoked and his bond put in suit. And it shall moreover be lawful for any person in the service of the United States, or for any Indian, to take and destroy any ardent spirits of wine found in the Indian country, except military supplies, as mentioned in this section; and by a subsequent act of Congress, imprisonment for a term of two years is also imposed upon all offenders."

As with almost any law, there was a loophole. In this case the catch was that alcohol sales to Indians were only illegal if they took place on Indian land, so traders went off the land and the sale became legal. Plus, if it was traded or used for barter, then the trader was technically not "selling" to the Indians. Despite seeing firsthand that selling whiskey to the Indians was bad for them spiritually, socially, and physically, traders continued to sell and barter with tribes all over the West. Even Beckwourth, a free black man who had gone west as a trapper and who had spent years among the Crow, acknowledged the harm alcohol caused, but explained that he was unable to resist making a profit from it. "Influenced by my persuasions, two hundred lodges of the Cheyennes started for the Platte, Bent and myself accompanying them. On our way thither we met one of my wagons, loaded with goods, on its way to the North Fork of the Platte. There was a forty-gallon cask of whisky among its contents, and, as the Indians insisted on having it opened, I brought it out of the wagon, and broached it. Bent begged me not to touch it, but to wait till we reached the fort. I was there for the purpose of making money, and when a chance offered, it was my duty to make the most of it. On that, he left me, and went to the fort. I commenced dealing it out, and, before it was half gone, I had realized sixteen horses and over two hundred robes."[18]

Beckwourth was equally disgusted with and compelled by how profitable the whiskey trading business was and the way in which it helped expand the American West. He wrote, "This trading whisky for Indian property is one of the most infernal practices ever entered into by man. Let the reader sit down and figure up the profits on a forty-gallon cask of alcohol, and he will be thunderstruck, or rather whisky struck. When disposed of, four gallons of water are added to each gallon of alcohol. In two hundred gallons there are sixteen hundred pints, for each one of which the trader gets a buffalo robe worth five dollars! The Indian women toil many long weeks to dress these sixteen hundred robes. The white trader gets them all for worse than nothing, for the poor Indian mother hides herself and her children in the forests until the effect of the poison passes away from the husbands, fathers, and brothers, who love them when they have no whisky, and abuse and kill them when they have. Six thousand dollars for sixty gallons of alcohol! Is it a wonder that, with such profits in prospect, men get rich who are engaged in the fur trade? or is it a miracle that the poor buffalo are becoming gradually exterminated, being killed with so little remorse that their very hides, among the Indians themselves, are known by the appellation of a pint of whisky?"[19]

For better or worse, by the mid-nineteenth century, the American West had changed and the United States stretched from ocean to ocean. The blend of people who lived there was continually changing. Whiskey had played a part in the great expansion, and its influence would continue to be felt into the twentieth century.

CHAPTER TWO

Nuts and Bolts:
From Grain to Liquid Gold

ALL WHISKEY IS DISTILLED FROM GRAIN. THE GRAIN IS MASHED and fermented, and then the alcohol is boiled off and collected through condensation. The mashing process converts the starch in the grains to sugar by using heat to activate the enzymes found in the grains. The fermentation process, adding water to the malt and letting it sit at a consistent temperature, results in an alcoholic "beer" that is further separated into ethyl alcohol and its byproducts through distillation. Early distillers commonly used a copper pot still to cook the "beer" and a cooling coil to condense the liquid that evaporated, collecting the end result in a large vessel.

It's a simple process, centuries if not millennia old, requiring relatively simple tools but also specific access to grain, clean water, and fuel for consistent heat sources. Early distillers relied on finding high-quality water sources—ideally good streams with naturally filtering limestone—and local farmers or their own labor to provide their ingredients. Wood or coal or another fuel for the fires stoked under the kettles was another requirement. The process was labor intensive, but the rewards could be enormous for entrepreneurs with the skill and know-how to convert grain to liquid gold.

The biggest technological improvement to the process in the nineteenth century came with the development of the continuous Coffey Still. Aeneas Coffey was granted Patent #5974 for his design of a two-column continuous still in 1830. This made great improvements in distillation speed and efficiency and increased the percentage of alcohol that collected for a given expenditure of energy.

The kind of grain that a whiskey product is distilled from affects its flavor, color, and name. Bourbon whiskey is made from a minimum of 51 percent corn, rye whiskey has 51 percent or more rye, and malt whiskey is predominantly malted barley. Both Irish and Scotch whiskey use barley; Scotch is 100 percent malted. Tennessee whiskey is bourbon that is chill-filtered via charcoal. Rye whiskey was generally produced in the East, where the grain grew best, and was a practical part of farming because it utilized leftover grains. George Washington's extensive still operation at Mount Vernon was based on the production of rye whiskey. The Monongahela rye of Pennsylvania was carried west by merchants and emigrants and could be found in mercantile stores and saloons on the frontier. Bourbon, because it's made predominantly from corn, was designated "America's Native Spirit" in a 1964 congressional resolution. A naturally sweeter product than rye, bourbon is typically associated with Kentucky, where corn production flourished and where bourbon may have got its name (see sidebar). Kentucky's reputation for making fine whiskey "grew with the new nation and spread across the United States and to the West as the Industrial Revolution facilitated travel and improved communications."[1]

How Bourbon Got Its Name

How bourbon came to be called *bourbon* is one of the oldest legends around—and perhaps one of the most spurious. One version of

Bininger's Traveler's Guide showing a bourbon advertising label with a man seated with a rifle passing a bottle to a standing man. Circa 1860s–1870s.

the story is that the name comes from Bourbon County, Kentucky, and that merchants in New Orleans found that shipments of whiskey carrying invoices indicating that they came from (the town of) Limestone, Bourbon County, Kentucky, were the most desirable. Their customers soon started asking for that "Bourbon County" whiskey, and the reference was eventually shortened to simply *bourbon whiskey*. There are two problems with this legend. The first is that in these early years of settlement there was limited trade with New Orleans (the round-trip took a year) and it is therefore unlikely that there were enough whiskey shipments invoiced to Limestone to catch the attention of New Orleanans. The second is that Limestone was part of Bourbon County for only a very brief time while Kentucky was still part of Virginia, and that by the time bourbon became a style of whiskey advertised in Kentucky newspapers, the town had been a part of Mason County for more than three decades. The oral tradition connecting the name to Bourbon County is strong, however. If there is any truth to it, most likely the bourbon–Bourbon County connection was made for pure marketing reasons after the 1803 Louisiana Purchase. It is also possible that the name came from river travelers drinking the aged whiskey of New Orleans on Bourbon Street and starting to ask for that "Bourbon Street whiskey." Whatever its origins, bourbon gave Kentucky a reputation for making fine whiskey.

Whiskey became a hot commodity and the revenue that would be collected by the federal government from distilled spirits across the nation was staggering. By 1860 several western states had their own distilleries. Iowa had eleven, twenty-two were in

A local saloon, The Bijou, receives a shipment of kegs in Round Pond, Oklahoma, 1894. Many saloons were referred to as "one-bit" and "two-bit" saloons because of their style and class. One bit equaled 12½ cents and two equaled 25 cents. This often described the decor and quality of whiskey the saloon sold. NATIONAL ARCHIVES

Missouri, and one was in Kansas. Maloney and Tilton, a distiller in St. Louis, Missouri, made a 95 percent above proof whiskey called Pike Peak's and advertised that it was expressly made for Utah, Santa Fe, New Mexico, and Pikes Peak, Colorado. California had nine distillers, Oregon one, Brigham Young's Utah now had six, and Washington had the most with twelve. According to the Wells' Commission's report: "Total in Pacific States and Territories, 28. Capital invested, $126,950; employed, 66; annual product in proof gallons, 836,200; value of annual product, $323,535."

Merchants, saloonkeepers, and emigrants heading west knew that whiskey was big business and that the market and the lack of law enforcement in the West had huge potential for profits. In attempting to regulate the whiskey trade, Congress actually created a vast whiskey supply that would aid in its association with the West. In 1865 the US Congress appointed a special commission, headed by David Wells, to review the measures taken to collect federal revenue during the Civil War and to see how they could revise the system. An alcohol tax was discussed—at length. In their report they noted, "that distilled spirits ought to contribute a very large proportion of the amount which the necessities of the country require shall be annually raised by internal taxation is, we believe, the almost unanimous sentiment of the whole country. It may, indeed, be considered as an axiom in political economy, that there is no article which creates a fairer subject for excise, and none which can be made to produce so much revenue with so little suffering to the taxpayer. . . . That distilled spirits can, furthermore, without detriment to any business interests of the country, be made to yield a revenue sufficiently large to lighten the burden on almost every other branch of industry, is an assertion that seems to scarcely need proof to substantiate." Because word had gotten out that the tax would only be levied on newly produced spirits, distillers worked until they were at capacity and beyond before the law took effect. When pioneers headed west immediately after the Civil War, they had access to plenty of cheap whiskey—the market had been glutted.[2]

In 1866 a commissioner appointed to study tax revenues reported numbers from across America: "The first tax imposed by Congress, under the present revenue system, on distilled spirits, was twenty cents per gallon. (Act of July 1, 1852.) The revenue derived from the same for the fiscal year ending June 30, 1863, was $3,229,991, which amount corresponds to a production of 16,149,955 proof gallons. The tax of twenty cents per gallon continued in force until March 7, 1864, when the rate was advanced to sixty cents per gallon. (Act of March 1, 1864.) The revenue derived from distilled spirits for the fiscal year ending June 30, 1864, under the two rates as above indicated, was $28,431,798. On the 1st of July, 1864, the tax on distilled spirits was raised to one dollar and fifty cents per proof gallon (act of June 30, 1864), which rate was further advanced on the 1st of January, 1865, to two dollars per proof gallon, the present rate of duty."[3]

The revenue derived from distilled spirits for the fiscal year ending June 1865 was $16,995,701 with the average taxable production of distilled spirits per year, from September 1, 1862, to June 30, 1865, at 40,537,371 gallons. Because the import duty on imported or foreign liquors like brandy, rum, and gin had been increasing, American-made whiskey was taking its place. The commissioner's report stated, "In fact, the imposition of the high rates of duty would seem to have nationalized this liquor as a beverage, every variety being sold under the common name of 'Bourbon,'" which essentially said that when government imposes a high tax on any product, it creates a market for illegal production.

Distillers and others in the business in Missouri enjoyed a good trade in the late 1860s and early 1870s. From the port city of St. Louis, they were able to ship their products to many western cities. Sam McCartney started his St. Louis whiskey business on June 4, 1867. His trademark was a single or double anchor on his barrels, and his reputation for good whiskey was something his family fought to keep. After he passed away ten years later, a cease and desist notice was placed in the newspaper: "The merchants of the South and West are respectfully notified, that no one has the right to make or sell whiskey under the brand DOUBLE ANCHOR or SINGLE ANCHOR or to use an anchor any way as a mark or brand [?] whiskey, unless licensed by the undersigned, as these brands are patented [?] belong exclusively to the heirs of Samuel McCartney (deceased). (Signed) Julia A. McCartney."[4]

Registering trademarks was one of the ways that distillers could ensure customers knew they were getting a genuine product. In the early 1870s over 7,700 trademarks had been filed with the US Patent Office. Many of the distillers were in Kentucky and Ohio, but there were quite a few west of the Mississippi. Some of them included San Francisco distillers H. Webster,

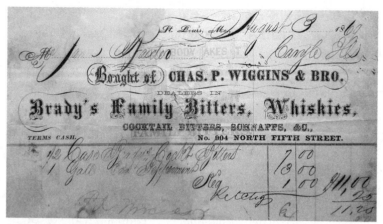

An invoice for bitters, dated August 3, 1869, from Charles B. Wiggans, who was a distributor in St. Louis. MISSOURI STATE HISTORY MUSEUM

who had trademark number 142 for "Kentucky Favorite 1864," Daniel Henarie with 209 for "J. F. Cutter," E. Martin with 210 for "Miller's Extra Old Bourbon," F. Chevalier with numbers 1049 and 2463 for "Castle," and Anson P. Hotaling with 5434 for "Death to Imitators."

St. Louis, Missouri, distillers included John L. Bernecker, who had number 207 for "L & B Eagle," J. A. Monks & Sons with 355 for "Douglass Elk-Horn Bourbon Whiskey" and 410 for their "Cane Spring Bourbon," William S. Stewart with 1459 for "Crown Royal," Derby & Day with 1490 for "Sunny South" and 1443 for "Superior Rectified Whiskey," and Torlina Express Co. with 2278 for "Grape Creek."

Famed early Mormon trader and overland stage mogul Benjamin Holladay opened a distillery near Weston, Missouri, in 1856, eventually turning the business over to his brother David. The distillery was on the site of a limestone spring first discovered by Lewis and Clark during their expedition. It was reported that their whiskey was well known as a genuine, handmade sour mash bourbon whiskey that was not adulterated. The reason for

Invoice for the St. Louis Distilling Company, from August 31, 1882.
MISSOURI STATE HISTORY MUSEUM

those words can be found in the rise of the rectifier in the world of whiskey.

Distillers like Holladay made whiskey from grains, water, and heat, while rectifiers "created whiskey" from the original product. Rectification is the process of redistilling whiskey or brandy or any alcoholic product to strip away all the congeners except ethanol to make neutral grain spirits. The noun "rectifier" referred to, and can still refer to, a business that would purchase bulk beverage alcohol and rectify or "fix" it to make it taste better to the consumer. Rectifiers used many techniques to do this: charcoal filtering, blending, redistilling, and adding color and flavor.

The difference between rectified spirits and the genuine article was the subject of a newspaper story that reported that whiskey was the most popular drink in the city and shed light on the process of making the spirit. The article referenced a newly published book called *Modern Compounding and Rectifying*. In it the authors included details on a popular cocktail and elixir known as Rock and Rye and how a compounder would make it. The article's headline read, "What'll You Have?" and began, "When a man answers the barkeeper's question: 'What will you have?' and gives his order, he might ask himself: 'What am I going to get?'"

The article went on to explain the secrets of the rectifier or compounder: "The first secret is that of making good sugar syrup. Of this, thirty pounds of rock candy, sifted as to remove the dust and boiled, will produce four gallons. Then the straight rye whiskey the rectifier takes one-half part of the whiskey he wishes to imitate and one-half of spirits. He adds a pint of prune juice to give the proper color and two drachms of the oil of bitter almonds. If he wishes to imitate bourbon, he omits the oil of almonds and substitutes one ounce of oil of corn. The rest of the recipe is the same. So, the man who calls for straight whisky may be getting the brand for which he asks or he may be getting this imitation which he could not distinguish from the original. As said, it depends upon the man and the place."[5]

Rock and Rye

Rock candy syrup was used to rectify rye whiskey into a product called Rock and Rye. This was a controversial beverage because not only was it offered as a cocktail in saloons, but it was also sold as a health tonic. Some mixologists recommended it to soothe a sore throat, but some just liked the way it tasted. The makers of one brand of Rock and Rye called Tolu, which was a popular health tonic in the late 1870s and early 1880s, claimed it could cure coughs, colds, sore throats, debilitated constitutions, weakness of the lungs, or consumption. The high alcohol content and lack of other active ingredients, of course, meant that the elixir wasn't actually effective, and it was banned in some areas. The *Bismarck*

Tribune reported in 1880, "TOLU ROCK AND RYE dealers are very scarce, Major Merrill having tendered them 'an indefinite leave of absence' from this reservation. Some of them have been bold enough not to accept, however, and are 'laying low' until the paymaster comes up, so that they can sell out their vile poison and then 'skip.' I think the presence of a U.S. marshal would have a very salutary effect about that time."[6]

In spite of its banishment from some locales, advertisements would appear all over the West for both the cocktail and the elixir known as Rock and Rye, under different brand names. The *Territorial Enterprise* in Virginia City, Nevada, reported, "Rock and Rye. Thomas Taylor & Co. have on sale in case or bulk Chelsey's celebrated 'Rock and Rye' whisky, which is having a great run in the Eastern states as a pleasant and efficacious remedy for coughs and colds. Those who have tried it say it is by no means bad to take, and make no 'wry' faces over it." The *New North-West* paper in Deer Lodge, Montana, wrote, "A favorite beverage of many Deer Lodgers is a compound known as 'Rock and Rye,' and, although a 'tanker,' we acknowledge at present a quantity of this liquid. It looks tempting, and should our cold continue—Bye and bye, Rock and Rye."

In the 1880s Rock and Rye was being sold as both a cocktail and as a health tonic, but those selling it as a tonic or elixir didn't have to pay the same tax as a distiller did. In July 20, 1881, the commissioner of the Internal Revenue addressed the sales of Rock and Rye in any form. He noted, "In view of the numerous preparations of the article generally known as 'Rock and Rye,' put up for sale throughout the United States, the following is

issued for your guidance. . . . " He basically
stated that Rock and Rye, either sold as whiskey, distilled spirits of any kind, or rock candy,
was now considered a compound liquor by
the federal government. Anyone selling these
products was now required to pay a special tax
as a rectifier, which was twenty cents per bottle instead four or five cents per bottle. Even if
an apothecary sold the mixture and labeled it
as medicine, it now had to pay the tax.[7]

Rectifiers, including those who made the concoction known
as "Rock and Rye," claimed they took poorly made whiskey and
made it more palatable—or claimed the health benefits of their
products—though sometimes they might add things that were
dangerous. In fact, a lack of real regulations meant that much
of the whiskey consumed in the late 1800s was downright dangerous. Coffin varnish, snake poison, tarantula juice, red liquor,
and a whole host of other euphemisms were used to describe
knockoff whiskey, but *rotgut* is the most well-known term. The
main ingredient in rotgut was not whiskey, but a clear substitute with additives. Safe rotgut was made with moonshine, plug
tobacco juice, and burnt sugar. The unsafe version was made with
kerosene. All were put into a barrel to "age" for a day or two,
and then it was strained and poured into bottles or decanters to
appear as whiskey. Most rectifiers used a colorless and odorless
version of whiskey that was sold cheap and combined the alcohol
with additives to make it look and taste more like rye or bourbon.
Suppliers made additives so the rectifiers could make their own
versions of whiskey. Burnt sugar coloring was one of the items
offered by bottle suppliers.

In 1879, when whiskey had been put under the government's
watch in bonded warehouses, the issue of safety was less of a
concern than profits and tax revenue. In 1885 a book called *The
Art of Blending and Compounding Liquors and Wines and Valuable*

Invoice for rectifiers Nelson and Mersman in St. Louis, dated February 15, 1865. MISSOURI STATE HISTORY MUSEUM

Information Concerning Whiskeys in Bond was published. The author, Joseph Fleischman, wrote, "The moment a barrel of liquor leaves the bonded warehouse, the first thing thought of, and done, is to reduce its cost. The blender knows how to make the bonded liquor produce a profit of 25 to 50 per cent, on the amount he paid for it, and frequently a great deal more. For the changes made by these cheapening processes neither the saloon-keeper nor his bartender is responsible; they can only offer for sale what they are able to purchase. The purchaser accepts the liquors he buys for what they are represented to be. The profits derived from this system of blending and mixing must be very great, judging from the large commissions that a rectifier is able to allow his agents for the sale of his products, amounting, sometimes, to $20 and $30 per barrel, and even more." He went on to explain how the bonding process worked: "All whiskeys, as soon as they are distilled, are placed under the supervision of a Government Agent in a bonded warehouse, where they are permitted to remain stored for three years, if not sooner withdrawn. Before a permit is granted for the withdrawal of whiskey from bond, a tax of 90 cents per gallon of proof spirits must be paid. . . . There will be usually during three years a shrinkage of 10 to 12 gallons in the contents of each barrel, and the increase in the percentage of proof of the remaining contents will be from 16 to 18 per cent. The tax for withdrawal at the end of three years is computed in the following manner: When a barrel of whiskey is placed in bond it contains full 45 gallons usually rather over; it would probably, in three years, suffer a shrinkage of 12 gallons; at the same time the increase of proof of the remainder would be about 16 per cent. Original bulk, say 45½ gallons. Shrinkage, 12 gallons. Leaving, 33½ wine gallons. 16% of 33½ equals 5½ increase of proof for a total of 38⅝ gallons, proof. On which the tax of 90 cents per gallon has to be paid, amounting to $34.95. In some cases, it may be that the shrinkage is greater than 12 gallons, but in that case the holder suffers, not the government." In 1885 forty-six gallons of whiskey cost, on average, $31.55 when calculated with the actual product, storage in bond, insurance, compounded interest, and shrinkage.[8]

⌇

In contrast to aged whiskey today, where the older the better seems to be the preference, new whiskey was preferred by many on the frontier. Fleischman wrote, "There is a general supposition that the older the whiskey the better it becomes. This is not altogether the fact, as whiskey that has been ten or fifteen years in the wood takes up too much of the tannin of the oak barrel, and is not as good a beverage as at earlier periods. There is always, however, a considerable quantity of old whiskey in the market, and it is generally used for blending with new whiskey, one or two gallons to the barrel, giving the new goods the taste and appearance of age. The cost of keeping whiskey for ten years is so increased, by shrinkage and the interest on the capital invested, that dealers do not, as a general rule, carry any great quantity of it, and when sold, it is usually filled up with high-proof spirits to bring it to the Government gauge and proof."

From the beginning, the makers, sellers, and consumers of straight whiskey considered the rectification process disreputable. Most rectifiers were distributors who purchased whiskey from distillers for resale to saloons, restaurants, and other retailers. Their suppliers were the hundreds of small country distilleries that dotted the landscape across Kentucky and other states.[9] The Bottled in Bond Act was enacted in 1897 because, until then, the government did not regulate what was put in whiskey bottles and sold to the public.

Kentucky distiller E. H. Taylor Jr. (whose great-uncle was President Zachary Taylor) was the leader of a lobby for governmental protection and regulation. At the time, Taylor owned several whiskey distilleries, including OFC, Old-Fashioned Copper, a distillery in Leestown, Kentucky. He was an expert marketer and entrepreneurial salesman who was passionate about the quality of his product, his branding, and educating the customer. Taylor was also one of the first distillers to create a showcase facility that welcomed visitors. Although financial strife caused him to sell his distillery to George T. Stagg in 1878, he remained dedicated to the production and protection of quality whiskey and played a significant role in the adoption of the Bottled in Bond Act.

The act was a significant regulatory reform that ensured that 100 percent of the liquid sold as single-malt whiskey was distilled in the same distilling season, by a single distiller, and that the spirit had been aged for a minimum of four years in a federally bonded warehouse. The warehouse could be a secured and totally separate space at the distiller's location, but it had to be inspected and approved by the federal government. Part of the act read: Packages of spirits of the same kind and only differing in proof, produced by the same distillery by the same distiller, during the same distilling season, may not be removed to the bottling house together; nor can spirits withdrawn for export and spirits withdrawn tax paid be in the bottling room at the same time. No material or substance of any kind other than pure water, can be added to the spirits during the process of bottling, nor can any substance or material be subtracted from the spirits, except that charcoal sediment or other like substances may be removed by straining them through cloth, felt or other like material; nor can any method or process be applied to alter or change in any way the original condition of character of the product, except as authorized by the statutes. The blank spaces in bottle stamps, which must cover the mouth of the bottle, must contain the registered distillery number, the real name of the bona-fide distiller, the State and district, the proof of the spirits, the year and distilling season, whether spring or fall, and the dates of the original Inspection or entry into bond, and of bottling.

Rectifiers understandably opposed the legislation and declared it gave an unfair advantage to the straight distillers. As competition grew, the rift widened between the two groups. The rectification process had become quite sophisticated since Lewis and Clark's time. The final product was now filtered through charcoal and when further purified became a very pure form of alcohol, known to the trade by such names as "cologne spirits" or "high-wines." Even after distillers rectified their product, businessmen who lacked a conscience and wanted to earn a tidy sum modified both rectified and pure whiskey with additives to extend their product. Many whiskey peddlers and saloon owners made their own version of whiskey. A "receipt" book contained a large volume of recipes for making all sorts of alcohol-based products. The books gave instructions on how to make medicine, vinegar, and several varieties of whiskey. They offered recipes made from the most popular whiskeys being sold and consumed in the West, including Monongahela, wheat, apple, old bourbon, imitation Irish, and imitation Scotch. They also supplied recipes for other alcohol like gin and brandy, but the main ingredient was whiskey.[10]

—◦—

By the end of the nineteenth century, many products labeled and sold as "whiskey" contained flavors and coloring agents designed to dilute whiskey to make it more profitable. The Coffey Still, which allowed distillers to redistill their product to or near neutral, made the production of rectified whiskey popular after 1831. By the mid-nineteenth century, a significant percentage of all spirits consumed in the United States was rectified whiskey. When made by more reputable rectifiers, the flavor of rectified whiskey was generally lighter and less harsh than straight whiskey, and because little if any of the typical blend was actually aged whiskey, rectified whiskeys were much less expensive. Rectified whiskey was also more consistent from batch to batch than all but the finest straight whiskey.

The grains of the Midwest made their way past the Mississippi River where pioneers, traders, bartenders, freighters, distillers, and more earned a living with some liquid gold.

CHAPTER THREE

The Rush Is On:
Pioneers and Settlements

By the middle of the nineteenth century, the days of rugged mountain men wandering untamed land past the Mississippi and Missouri Rivers were quickly becoming history. Their stories were replaced by those of the brave pioneers who followed their trails. Men and women were determined to settle and tame a new land while taking advantage of all the opportunities it might afford. The mountain men who had spent decades at high elevations and on the lower prairies were no longer able to make a living hunting and trapping and exploring, so some changed tactics, earning their living guiding often clueless and ill-prepared emigrants across the West.

Early reports from pioneers who were settling the West excited many easterners, some of whom sold off a large portion of their belongings and excitedly packed their wagons as they prepared to traverse the plains and prairies in search of a new life. Many adventurous souls dreamed of a place with wide-open spaces, where neighbors were few, and the land was theirs for the taking—in some cases. Their reasons for making the life-altering choice to emigrate were as diverse as the travelers themselves. American, European, Asian, and other pioneers were all bent on taking advantage of new opportunities. Some were looking for a new start, running from a shady past, or seeking their fortunes.

Starting in the 1830s, enticing firsthand accounts of the bountiful natural resources and land to be had for settlement had already lured thousands to journey to the frontier, but by the early 1840s, a flood of humans, animals, and material goods were about to engulf the frontier. Shortly after John C. Frémont undertook his first of four expeditions across the Great Plains and through the Rocky Mountains, his glowing reports began to entice emigrants to move to the Oregon Territory. In 1845, in response to those reports and anticipating the deluge of settlers about to head west, newspaper editor John O'Sullivan penned the famous phrase "Manifest Destiny" in his *Democratic Review*. He wrote that all Americans had a God-given right to occupy the entire North American continent. Once the Mexican-American War settled ownership over the western territories at the end of the 1840s, the move to inhabit the West took hold in the American imagination and emigration began in earnest.

Individuals and groups headed west with their own stories and their own traditions. In the case of the religious group known as the Latter-day Saints, leader Brigham Young opened up a settlement in the valley of the Great Salt Lake in what is now Utah in 1847, hoping to find refuge from the persecution the sect faced in the East. Ten years later, between 1856 and 1860, nearly three thousand members of the faith would push handcarts halfway across the country, walking to what is now Utah with their belongings.

Still other trails were blazed by the fortune hunters enticed by the gold strikes in California and Nevada—and by the merchants and other entrepreneurs who followed in their wake, intent on profiting from the miners' work in the placer mines. Even though

Millions of people traveled west from 1860 to 1900 in search of a better life. Most proclaimed it Manifest Destiny to exploit the resources of the West. The trek was rough and rugged, dangerous, and uncertain. With only a few established towns, emigrants had few options, and that led to whiskey's enhanced value as a resource. Circa 1873. LIBRARY OF CONGRESS

emigrants had been traversing the West since the early 1800s, the phrase "FREE LAND!" was a hook that caught the attention of many. It was heard across America when the Homestead Act was passed in 1862 and enacted on January 1, 1863. The act provided for a threefold homestead acquisition process where a US citizen or intended citizen who had never borne arms against the US government was permitted to file an application and lay claim to 160 acres of surveyed government land. To gain ownership, a homesteader had to live on the land for five years and improve it by building a twelve-by-fourteen-foot dwelling and growing crops. If the hardworking pioneer made it after five years, he or she could file for a patent (or deed of title) by submitting proof of

Boot & Co. (general store) in Colorado, circa 1800s. "Meat market, storage, groceries, liquors and cigars." NEW YORK PUBLIC LIBRARY DIGITAL COLLECTIONS

residency and showing the completed required improvements to a local land office.

Homestead lots were available in some eastern states, but most people in the East and Europe felt the draw of the wide-open West and preferred it over living in big-city tenements. They chose to settle in places like Colorado, Dakota Territory, Montana Territory, Kansas, and Nebraska.

The Homestead Act was one of the greatest events to influence the settling of the West and expanding America. People now had a choice on where to settle, and many chose to traverse the unknown regions of the West and face the dangers of weather, the unknown company of native peoples, and the lack of basic necessities. Because of the harsh conditions of windy open plains, swollen rivers, mind-numbing blizzards, and lack of timber in many places, most people didn't last the five years. But those who did claimed their land. January 1, 1863, was the first day that claims could be filed, and over four hundred people did just that.

To get to their land, many pioneers took their own wagons and traveled with several other families in what was called an emigrant train. These groups of intrepid men, women, and children followed the trails that had been painstakingly carved out by the mountain men and the lure of free land and opportunity. The most well-known route taken by these pioneers was the Oregon Trail, which came into use in the 1840s. Each spring thousands of emigrants arrived in Independence, Missouri, intent on embarking on the two-thousand-mile journey to the Pacific Northwest. They "jumped off" from Independence and followed the Platte River through the South Pass of the Rocky Mountains and then northwest to the Colombia River and into the Willamette Valley near Fort Dalles in present-day Oregon, and they carried whiskey with them. It was at this point where most pioneers were excited, happy, and a little nervous. Whiskey would come into play as the journey grew long, when loneliness and illness descended and blanketed the excitement.

Whiskey was a trade good and a social lubricator, and was liberally used for its supposed medicinal purposes. When Chestina Bowker Allen traveled to Kansas Territory from Massachusetts with her husband and children in 1854–1855, she witnessed the effects that whiskey had on snakebite victims: "At eve as Abbie was going after the cows that were in sight, she stepped on a snake, it bit her leg and run off, we were much frightened as we did not know what kind it was. I sucked the bites it had bit twice, washed it in saleratus, put on sweet oil and gave her whiskey. No signs of poison appeared."

Having a good supply of whiskey to start the journey was wise, because with the exception of small operations, there was no large-scale whiskey distilling past the Mississippi River. Fortunately for the pioneers heading west, they could load up an ample supply of whiskey from distillers in the East or in the Midwest. The hamlet of Soda Springs, Idaho, was conveniently situated along the Oregon Trail and afforded weary pioneers some much-needed refreshment. It had clear and bubbling natural springs, which the native peoples and emigrants alike frequented. By the early 1850s, some emigrants taking the trail had settled there and turned trading with other emigrants into a profitable venture. Pioneer Sarah Sutton arrived at Soda Springs and noted that there was a blacksmith shop and two or three traders. She penned, "The traders had no flour to sell, but when they had it, they sold it for $25 a hundred. ...Whiskey was 1.50 a pint, cheese 50 cents a pound."[1]

The wagon trains were popular because there was safety in numbers and many groups shared provisions. The whiskey or brandy that was carried along and frequently used to care for the sick among the group or enjoyed as a nightcap was transported in casks or barrels large enough to be shared among all the members of a train, but some travelers kept a small amount in their private caches, as well. When the emigrants needed a refill, they might find a trading post, stage stop, or nearby fort where they could purchase spirits, but they would have paid dearly for replenishment.

In the case of the Latter-day Saints' settlement in the Salt Lake Valley of Utah, Brigham Young, who had taken on the leadership of the church after the murder of its founder, Joseph Smith, was not only a religious leader but also a shrewd businessman. In addition to many other businesses that he and the other settlers started, Young began distilling his own whiskey from wheat grown in the area around the Great Salt Lake. While corn and rye were the typical ingredients used in distilling whiskey, the availability of wheat made it a common choice in the West.

Within a few short years of their arrival, the Mormons, as they were known, had started several manufacturing businesses, including wool-carding machines, cloth and blanket factories, tanneries, a pottery for coarse brown-ware, machine shops, and iron and brass foundries, in addition to other basic businesses. Because a tannery was one of the first enterprises started, many things produced by the Mormons were given the nickname of "Valley Tan," including their whiskey.[2]

In 1853 the Mormons were well on their way to establishing a solid community when a new business opportunity presented itself. It started with the purchase of a machine that would convert beetroots into sugar, but all they produced was gallons of useless syrup. The frugal Mormons did not want to waste the syrup, so Brigham Young found a new use for the syrup—they distilled it.[3]

The beetroot alternative did not sit well with Mormon John Hyde, who was church elder under Young. He left the church in disgust and in 1857 wrote, "It [beetroot] could not be converted into sugar, it could not be used as molasses, he would distill it into RUM. Accordingly, this bad molasses was converted into worse liquor; and, after coloring it with burnt sugar and flavoring it with green tea, the delicious compound was sold by Brigham's adopted son, W. C. Staines, at the very reasonable price of eight dollars per gallon. By this ingenious operation quite a little sum was clearly gained, and it was slyly hinted that the proceeds were expended in helping to build the Temple. If it be true, and I confess I doubt it, it was cementing the walls of the Lord's house with human drunkenness and human degradation!"[4]

Hyde also noted there were several distilleries in the area and commented,

Nor was this by any means the only distillery in Salt Lake City, although, in order that the Church might regulate such matters, and perhaps to prevent competition, all the other distilleries were prohibited from making any liquor during the above saintly speculation. Dr. Clinton had a distillery producing the most infamous decoction of wheat. He was sent on a mission, and the Church purchased his distillery from his wives for its own private working. Hugh Moon has quite an extensive one in operation at Salt Lake. During the life of Dr. Richards, a prophet, seer, revelator, and editor, his little cart used to make daily visits to Moon's distillery, and take thence from a quart to a gallon of liquor; and J. D. Ross, now preaching in England, was sent away from Salt Lake as a missionary, almost entirely because he was overbold in asserting that Moon made the spirit that inspired the leaders in the "Deseret News." There is also another distillery in the city, and several in other parts of the Territory. Brigham has a city named after himself, on Box-elder creek, sixty miles north of Salt Lake City. Even in this holy place, a man named Clarke produces a liquid he calls and the people buy for whiskey. At Ogden City there is another such distillery; another at Provo, and so on throughout the whole Territory. Added to the hogsheads of wash produced at these Mormon factories, each of the merchants imports hundreds of gallons every year, and, as a general rule, although not arriving till June, all is sold out by Christmas. . . .

Despite the distilleries in and around Salt Lake, Hyde found positive things to say about his brethren: "Hence, the Mormons are a jovial people, hospitable, dance and song, and dram-loving. Their kindness to strangers, their general affection for each other, their devoted obedience to the authorities, their bitter animosity to all Gentiles, their rigid adherence to ceremonies, their lax code

Waitresses sit on the bar with a dog at a 1900s saloon near Ogden, Utah.
UTAH STATE HISTORICAL SOCIETY

of morals, and yet precise restriction to that established code, arrests the attention of all observers. One thing must be also remarked. There is less public drunkenness, no houses of ill fame, no public bad women, less monstrous crime among the Mormons than in any other community of equal size."[5]

Josiah Gibbs, born in Nauvoo, Illinois, was more forthcoming about the Mormons and their Valley Tan whiskey. Josiah's father was a follower of Joseph Smith and Brigham Young and had taken his family to Salt Lake City to settle. Smith, the founder of the Church of Latter-day Saints, had set an early example for his followers when it came to whiskey and drinking—and selling alcohol. When Smith moved into his new Illinois mansion in 1843, he allowed his follower Orrin Porter Rockwell Jr. to set up a saloon nearby. The Americana Society's newspaper reported on the business, "Since a general ordinance prohibited hotels from selling intoxicants, the above license gave the prophet's hotel a whiskey monopoly. Not being satisfied with this, Smith, later secured from the municipal authorities, the passage of an ordinance, authorizing him to sell whiskey but prohibiting others, except by his license."[6]

Josiah Gibbs, in his later years, wrote a book about his experience with the Mormon faith. He penned, "During the fifty-one years in which I have intimately associated with the Mormon people, I have seen all the lights and shadows of Mormonism; I have partaken of the good there is in it, and have drunk to the very dregs of its bitterness. But there is no feeling, other than that of kindness toward a people whose only fault is unquestioning credulity. And now for the motive for the publication of this book. After I had been excommunicated, I began a careful study of the so-called 'revelations,' and of the early history of Joseph Smith and of the church which he founded. Except as to the *Book of Mormon*, I had taken little interest in them since my mission in England. Months were consumed in a close and unbiased investigation. Those things which appealed to me as truths during my boyhood, became glaringly inconsistent under the analysis to which I subjected them, and I was surprised that I had not heretofore discovered the thinly disguised deception. The new verdict was arrived at by a process of reasoning. It was the operation of a mature mind versus the impressions of childhood."

Gibbs, writing years later after he was excommunicated by the church, was outraged at the hypocrisy espoused by the Mormon leaders when it came to whiskey sales and consumption. "And whatever vice and crime arose from the sale and consumption of intoxicants during the period under discussion, is justly chargeable to the Mormon leaders. Instead, however, of bringing their unappealable dictum to bear on the side of temperance and decent morals, the Prophet Brigham became a distiller of whiskey and other intoxicants, and high priests were the wholesale and retail distributors." Gibbs went on to say that "on July 29, 1854, John Mellon, another good Saint, asked for a renewal of his saloon license. Mellon had been guilty of selling liquor to children, and his license was revoked until he made 'satisfaction to the city council.' In those days, 'making satisfaction' generally consisted of going before the Saints assembled in the capacity of ward meetings, and asking forgiveness, and there is little doubt that Brother Mellon took that course, for, on August 12th, he secured permission to continue his business of making drunkards of the 'Saints of the Most High,' and that, too, under the quasi benediction of the prophets of the 'only true church of Christ on earth!' During the years 1851 to 1857, the Prophet Brigham was Governor of Utah. And under the authority of the territorial legislature; Governor Young was the sole supervisor of the whiskey business in Utah."[7]

Even Mark Twain wrote about Young and his whiskey: "The exclusive Mormon refresher; valley tan is a kind of whisky, or first cousin to it; is of Mormon invention and manufactured only in Utah. Tradition says it is made of [imported] fire and brimstone. If I remember rightly, no public drinking saloons were allowed in the kingdom by Brigham Young, and no private drinking permitted among the faithful, except they confined themselves to Valley Tan."

Sir Richard Burton would report of the beverage: "The whisky of Utah Territory, unlike the Monongahela or rye of Pennsylvania, and the Bourbon, or maize brandy of Kentucky, is distilled from wheat only; it is, in fact, the korn schnapps of the trans-Rheine region. This 'Valley Tan,' being generally pure. . . ."[8]

Joseph Smith's onetime bodyguard and bartender Orrin Porter Rockwell Jr. eventually ended up with Brigham Young. Author Richard Burton recalled Rockwell's fondness for Valley Tan when he met him. He wrote,

> *Porter Rockwell was a man about fifty, tall and strong, with ample leather leggins overhanging his huge spurs, and the saw-handles of two revolvers peeping from his blouse. His forehead was already a little bald, and he wore his long grizzly locks after the ancient fashion of the United States,*

plaited and gathered up at the nape of the neck; his brow,
puckered with frowning wrinkles, contrasted curiously with
his cool, determined gray eye, jolly red face, well touched
up with "paint," and his laughing, good-humored mouth.
He had the manner of a jovial, reckless, devil-may-care
English ruffian. The officers called him Porter, and preferred
him to the "slimy villains" who will drink with a man and
then murder him. After a little preliminary business about
a stolen horse, all conducted on the amiable, he pulled out a
dollar, and sent to the neighboring distillery for a bottle of
Valley Tan. The aguardiente was smuggled in under a cloth,
as though we had been respectables in a Moslem country, and
we were asked to join him in a "squar drink," which means
spirits without water. The mode of drinking was peculiar.
Porter, after the preliminary sputation, raised the glass
with cocked little finger to his lips, with a twinkle of the eye
ejaculated "Wheat!" that is to say, "good," and drained the
tumbler to the bottom: we acknowledged his civility with a
"here's how," and drank Kentucky-fashion, which in English
is midshipman's grog. Of these "squar drinks" we had at least
four, which, however, did not shake Mr. Rockwell's nerve,
and then he sent out for more.

Many other establishments sprang up across the West to
accommodate the needs of the settlers. At a ranch on the South
Platte in what is now Nebraska, storekeepers placed boards across
two barrels to give the appearance of a frontier bar. Firsthand
accounts described the whiskey sold at this bar as "a decoction of
some of the vilest stuff under the name of 'old Bourbon whisky'
that ever irrigated the throat of the worst old toper. To a few
gallons of 'sod-corn juice,' it was said that the proprietors of the
place would add a quantity of tobacco and some poisonous drugs,
and thus manufacture a barrel of the worst 'rot-gut' ever produced.
The vile liquid was sold to thirsty customers at enormous prices."[9]

Early pioneer and author Richard Burton recalled replenishing his whiskey supply at Fort Bridger when he traveled overland with the Daniel Robinson Company. He penned, "Arrived at Fort Bridger, our first thought was to replenish our whisky-keg: its emptiness was probably due to the 'rapid evaporation in such an elevated region imperfectly protected by timber;' but, however that may be, I never saw liquor disappear at such a rate before. Pur parenthèse, our late friends the officials had scarcely been more fortunate: they had watched their whiskey with the eyes of Argus, yet, as the driver facetiously remarked, though the quantity did not diminish too rapidly, the quality lost strength every day."[10]

Frank Root, an overland stage driver, described the ability of one of his acquaintances to procure whiskey. "Another driver on the Platte was known as 'Whisky Jack.' As might naturally be inferred from the name, he had little use for water except for his infrequent ablutions. But he had achieved a reputation in another way; the fellow could get away with more double-rectified, copper-distilled, sod-corn juice than any other man who sat on the box of a four- or six-horse stage-coach. Notwithstanding his prodigious appetite for whiskey, he was a kind, good-natured fellow."

The stories of whiskey along the trail are numerous—some humorous and some deadly. Mormon emigrant Peter Olsen Hanson wrote in his diary about an incident that caused him great distress: "Another time while on the plains the following unpleasant incident took place. The seven first teams in the company were Br.[other] Kimballs, Capt. Egan drove the first which was a mule team. I drove an ox team, and the other five teamsters were [mere] boys. In one of the wagons was a barrel of whiskey, and one day 3 of the boys had bored the barrel and let out some whiskey and drank, this was and the Captain noticed their been acting a little silly and found that the bared barrel had been bored, and thinking that I must know of the doings and have shared in the fun, he kept from speaking to me a whole week, not until one day he had an occasion to come right close to me, I spoke and asked him what was the reason for his not speaking to me, when he smiled and told me what had occurred and how he had [thought] that I must be guilty with the boys. I told him it was the first news to me, nevertheless I remembered seeing them uncommon playful one day, but had not mistrusted any such thing as w[h]isky drinking, and he said he [k]new I would not lie, and he had ful[l] confidence in me again. I afterwards found that the two youngest boys were ignorant of the mischief as well as me. These youngsters caused me a good deal of unpleasantness, as he held me some-ought responsible for their conduct."[11]

Another emigrant heading west, William Audley Maxwell, wrote about whiskey experiences and a trading post along the California Trail. He came upon an enterprising gentleman who had set up a whiskey trading post near Humboldt Springs. Maxwell wrote, "Not far from the spring was situated a rude shack, known as 'Black's Trading Post.' This establishment was constructed of scraps of rough lumber, sticks, stones and cow-hides. With Mr. Black were two men, said to be his helpers—helpers in what, did not appear. The principal stock in trade was a barrel of whisky—reported to be of very bad quality—some plug tobacco, and—not much else. Black's prices were high. A sip from the barrel cost fifty cents. It was said to be an antidote for alkali poisoning. Some of our men visited this emporium of the desert, and there they found 'Jim' Tooly. The barrel had been tapped in his behalf, and he was loquacious; appearing also to be quite 'at home' about the Post. His two companions of our recent acquaintance were not there. The 'antidote' was working; Tooly was in good spirits, and eloquent. He did not appear to recognize those of our people who were visiting the place; but they knew him. There were other persons present from the camps of two or three companies of emigrants, but strangers to us, who were also stopping for the night at the margin of the Sink. Tooly assumed an air of comradeship toward all, addressing various individuals as 'Partner' and 'Neighbor'; but his obvious willingness to hold the center of the stage made it clear that he deemed himself the important personage of the community."[12]

The desire for whiskey often caused people to commit criminal acts. The summer of 1852 was not kind to the emigrants traveling the Oregon Trail with the Robert Wimmer Company. Wimmer was in charge of about seventy wagons and 250 faithful souls. Ten-year-old Orson Hyde Elliott was one of the children heading for Utah and later wrote about his experiences. They left Iowa in early July, but before they reached the Black Hills in Dakota Territory, they decided to split up the group. While it was generally safer to travel in large groups, the lack of grass and too many stock animals proved difficult for Wimmer's group. So they decided to split the group to allow for better grazing and survival. Orson Hyde Elliott captured what happened:

> The grass dried up as the summer advanced, and it was discovered that our company of one hundred wagons and a thousand cattle and horses was entirely too big to travel together with comfort. An Englishman named T[homas]. D[unlop]. Brown, who had former been a merchant at Council Bluffs, was traveling with us. Besides his family, he had a large stock of merchandise, consisting of dry goods, groceries and whisky. Those in authority, as soon as some of the Twelve Apostles came along, called a meeting and decided to divide up the train. Before dividing up, some of the brethren lacking in the spirit of God, thought they would make up the difference by tapping old Brown's whisky barrels. One night they did so, and not having the proper tools to carry out their plans successfully, they bored into the hind end of a wagon into the barrel. Not having a faucet, most of the whisky was lost on the ground. Whisky was worth a dollar a pint, so they caught as much as they could in pails, but only a small portion was thus saved.

In due time Brother Brown discovered the theft, and he straightway called a council of war. A day or two afterwards the presiding elders and some of the Twelve Apostles arrived, when a meeting was called and an investigation was ordered. As they were unable to discover the culprits, they were obliged to content themselves by putting on trial those who were on guard that night. However, they were not able to fasten the guilt upon anyone in particular. The Twelve Apostles, or those in charge, tried to satisfy Brother Brown by denouncing the parties who had been mean enough to steal his whisky, and there they rested. But Brown was not to be so pacified. He refused to travel with such an ungodly set, withdrew from the company, and when he got to Salt Lake he apostatized. Our company got into all sorts of dissensions. The spirit of God did not seem to abide with them after they stole Brown's whisky, so they broke up in a row. It was "every fellow for himself, and the devil take the hindmost." [13]

While wagons were the only vehicles by which pioneers could travel to all points west early on, they would later cross the country via stagecoach or train or both. One such individual wrote a letter back to the East about his adventure in 1865. Demas Barnes traveled by train to Atchison, Kansas, where he boarded a Concord coach and headed "overland" to begin his life in the West. While stopped in Denver, he wrote about the rough conditions and bad whiskey:

I had not deemed it a great undertaking for another to cross the continent overland, but when I sit here midway, at the foot of the Rocky Mountains, the habits of my life changed— all connection with the accumulated interests of many years of toil suspended, social ties sundered, kind friends and loved ones far behind me, with rugged hills, parched deserts, and lonely wastes far, far ahead, I do feel it is a great undertaking for me—for any one. Many friends said they envied me my trip, would themselves like to go, etc. I do not doubt their sincerity—I have thought so myself—but I beg to undeceive them. It is not a pleasant, but it is an interesting trip. The conditions of one man's running stages to make money, while another seeks to ride in them for pleasure, are not in harmony to produce comfort. Coaches will be overloaded, it will rain, the dust will drive, baggage will be left to the storm, passengers will get sick, a gentleman of gallantry will hold the baby, children will cry, nature demands sleep, passengers will get angry, the drivers will swear, the sensitive will shrink, rations will give out, potatoes become worth a gold dollar each, and not to be had at that, the water brackish, the whiskey abominable, and the dirt almost unendurable.

Barnes continued his lamentations:

I have just finished six days and nights of this thing; and I am free to say, until I forget a great many things now very visible to me, I shall not undertake it again. Stop over nights? No you wouldn't. To sleep on the sand floor of a one-story sod or adobe hut, without a chance to wash, with miserable food, uncongenial companionship, loss of seat in a coach until one comes empty, etc., won't work. A through-ticket and fifteen inches of seat, with a fat man on one side, a poor widow on the other, a baby in your lap, a bandbox over your head, and three or four more persons immediately in front, leaning against your knees, makes the picture, as well as your sleeping place, for the trip—but of all this when I come to it.[14]

Demas Barnes was not exaggerating the exorbitant cost of goods in his reminiscences. One of the stage stations where he would have stopped was Ben Holladay's in LaPorte, Colorado.

Travel by stagecoach was uncomfortable, dusty, and often very crowded. Circa mid- to late 1800s. UTAH STATE HISTORICAL SOCIETY

Frank Root was an overland stage driver who recalled the cost of goods there: "Eggs cost $1.25 to $1.50 per dozen, potatoes were sixteen cents per pound, butter was $1 per pound, and whiskey was twenty-five cents. Those who wanted to have a supply of whiskey for the next portion of their journey visited a local liquor house. They took their bottles to the back room of the store and had them filled. This was a little more difficult during the cold months, when the owner had to stick a red-hot poker in the bung hole of the whiskey barrel that had frozen in order to let the drink flow."[15]

Root also commented on the state of the cities that sprang up in the West and accommodated the tastes of some emigrants: "I shall never forget the first time I saw Denver. . . . There was considerable Mexican whisky disposed of in Denver in the early '60s. At the Mexican gambling houses on Blake street, where one of the favorite games they played was 'Spanish monte,' the vile whisky, some of which drank by the overland-stage drivers, was by them given the very appropriate name of 'Taos lightning.'"[16]

Brigham Young and his brethren had demonstrated that strong drink could be made from the bounty of the land, through their use of wheat and sugar beets to produce whiskey and rum. Both distilling and rectifying whiskey required skill. And both were lucrative businesses.

Before the completion of the transcontinental railroad, whiskey was transported to western trading posts, settlements, towns, and cities by ship and stagecoach. The big rivers like the Missouri and Mississippi were key to the transport of goods needed in the West, as were smaller rivers like the deep Osage River, which flowed through Missouri between the Lakes of the Ozarks and the Missouri River. A sternwheel steamship named the *Tom Stevens* carried goods on the Osage from merchant J. F. McKernan & Co. in Osage City, Missouri, to St. Thomas, Missouri. One bill of lading included three bars of iron, one box of nails, one keg of whiskey, and other miscellaneous cargo. The freight was assessed at twenty-five cents per one hundred pounds. The whiskey keg weighed seventy-five pounds, and the delivery included fifty cents for freight and ten cents for commission.[17] In the 1860s it was common in western towns to see advertisements in newspapers about the latest shipments coming from eastern manufacturers. Wholesalers would list the name of the ship, how many barrels they received, and where it had come from to bring in customers.

St. Louis, Missouri, also had its share of distillers, and, according to *Gould's St. Louis Directory, 1875*, the city had made great advances in malt and distilled liquors. Based on the records of the Internal Revenue Division, the quantity of whiskey that was "officially reported" had increased from about 1,600,000 gallons in 1870 to 2,200,000 gallons in 1874 and was taxed at about seventy cents per gallon of whiskey. It's almost certain that more whiskey was actually produced and sold in St. Louis in 1874 because the tax being paid by distillers wasn't being reported accurately. Distillers were buying their required tax stamps, but they were reusing them rather than purchasing them at the rate they made their product.

John McDonald, the regional supervisor of the Internal Revenue Division, was aware that the tax stamps were being reused, which meant legitimate tax money was not making it back to Washington, DC. There were, in fact, three different stamps required. One was applied once the whiskey was made and put into the government warehouse; another, called the "tax-paid" stamp, was applied after the whiskey was taken from the warehouse and was sold; and another that would be applied when the whiskey was rectified. Each time the stamp was applied, it was supposed to be done under the supervision of a government official. *Frank Leslie's Illustrated Newspaper* reported how easily the system could be gamed: "A gauger measures every barrel, and the storekeeper sees that the stamps are put on at the right time and in the right places. In this way, 'crooked whisky' was not different from any other kind in the making, but existed alone on the books of government officials. Sometimes the same stamps would be used two, three and four times. For instance, Bevis & Fraser would purchase five hundred worth of tax-paid stamps. They would put these on so many barrels of whisky, or high wines, at their distillery or warehouse, and send them up to their rectifying house, where the stamps would be removed and returned, instead of being destroyed. The official has them so prepared that they could be put on and off without injury."[18]

Efforts to work around the regulation and taxation became known as the "whiskey ring." In his book, *Secrets of the Great Whiskey Ring*, McDonald asserted that President Ulysses S. Grant and his cronies were behind the ring as part of their effort to get Grant reelected. He wrote, "The great whiskey frauds culminating in 1875, are a part of the history of American politics. No ring was ever before formed embracing such a gigantic scope and including among its chief instigators and membership, such distinguished

Government officials. The original intention of the organizers, adopting suggestions from the highest authority in the land, was to make the ring co-extensive with the nation, with headquarters in all the large cities, for the purpose of raising a campaign fund with which to advance the interests of President Grant in his aspirations for a second term. So far as my personal knowledge extends, the money received from the distillers and rectifiers was used according to the original intention of the members, until Grant's re-election, when, the purposes of the organization having been accomplished, but with the management of the colossal fraudulent undertaking thoroughly in hand, it was decided to continue the appropriation of the revenue and to make the members of the ring the beneficiaries of the fund. During congressional and municipal campaigns, however, a part of this fund was always used in the interests of the Republican candidates."[19]

When McDonald was appointed as Internal Revenue supervisor and sent to St. Louis, he recalled, "Immediately after assuming charge of the revenues of Missouri I had a conversation with Wm. McKee, senior proprietor of the *Missouri Democrat*, in which he admitted that his opposition to the President was caused by Grant's persistency in appointing persons to office in St. Louis contrary to his (McKee's) expressed wishes, and against the best policy of the party in the state. He was especially bitter against Ford, the collector, and asserted that he was entitled to the benefits bestowed upon the party by his paper. Several other conversations occurred between us in which contingencies were provided for."[20]

McDonald received a tip about the local revenue collector and a distillery in the early part of April 1870 from Acting Commissioner Douglass. Douglass had received this note from B. D. Simpson: "You had better examine Mr. [C. W.] Ford's affairs at once, as well as L. Card's distillery; if you do so, as it ought to be done, you will find something which will astonish you."

McDonald said of this letter, "In this connection it is proper that the reader understand the fact that nearly every distillery in the district was, at that time, libeled and shut up, and the revenue was coming in at an exceedingly slow rate; but I at once acted upon the suggestion of this letter and thoroughly investigated Mr. Ford's [collector] books, and also the distillery." In another investigation, McDonald explained how he discovered frauds that were being perpetrated by Ford: "In the investigation, I prosecuted at Ulrici's distillery (formerly run by Card & Lawrence, as referred to in Simpson's letter of information,) a most glaring fraud was unearthed, viz. the discovery of 48,000 bushels of grain, which had been used for distillation and unaccounted for to the Government. The magnitude of this fraud was equal to stealing directly from the Government the sum of $117,600, and I at once accused Mr. Ford of guilty knowledge in the disposition of that money. After a season of skillful evasion Mr. Ford admitted the frauds, and exhibited the deepest humility and remorse of conscience."[21]

It was after this discovery when McKee told McDonald that he wanted to keep Ford as the collector. McDonald claimed that McKee suggested he find a ring leader. "For some time before this McKee had made suggestions to me about organizing a ring among the revenue officials in St. Louis, to derive profits from illicit distilling." Ford was not agreeable to this because he and McKee didn't get along. McDonald claims the matter was presented to President Grant. "The matter was then laid before President Grant, together with an explanation of McKee's opposition to the administration. Soon afterwards Ford signified his willingness to meet and arrange details with McKee, which, (I can state with only circumstantial proof,) was caused by instructions from the President to Mr. Ford. Having come to an understanding, arrangements were completed by which McKee, Ford and myself were to control all the federal appointments in Missouri, the Senators of that time, (Hon. Frank Blair and Hon. Carl Schurz,) not being in sympathy with the administration, and were consequently ignored by the President. The revenue was honestly collected and returned until the fall of 1871, when, at the suggestion of Mr. McKee, one Conduce G. Maguire was imported from Cincinnati to manage the illicit distilling, and to arrange for the collection of the assessments to be made on the distillers and rectifiers. . . . I went to Washington myself and remained there until I had procured the release of all the libeled distilleries. During my stay in Washington, I received the following letter from John A. Joyce, my private secretary, who was well acquainted with the purposes of the King and that the President was to share its profits."[22]

In his book, *A Checkered Life*, accused and convicted conspirator John Joyce told of how he and the other accused conspirators were rounded up in the spring and summer of 1876. The alleged conspirators in St. Louis were put on trial before Treat and Dillon, who were the US judges. The most prominent in the case was John McDonald; John Joyce; William McKee, editor and proprietor of the *Globe-Democrat*; Conduce Maguire, collector of Internal Revenue; William O. Avery, chief clerk of the US Treasury Department; and General O. E. Babcock, private and official secretary of President Grant. The government also indicted deputy collectors, gaugers, storekeepers, distillers, and rectifiers. It is interesting to note that in his book, Joyce only refers to McDonald as "Supervisor" and never by name.

According to Joyce, "the prosecution of the so-called whiskey conspirators, from the beginning to the end, cost the government one million dollars; and in the loss of taxes from idle distilleries and whiskey houses, it suffered a loss of two million more making in all a three-million-dollar robbery from the vaults of the treasury by a set of official conspirators who acted, not for the enforcement of the law, but to promote their own personal and political ambition. After eight years, where are the men who made such loud boasts in the whiskey prosecutions? Many of their victims died in poverty."[23]

Secretary of the Treasury Benjamin Bristow is credited with breaking up the Whiskey Ring. Bristow claimed it was a politically organized group of businessmen and politicians who were defrauding the federal government of tax revenue, and it centered around St. Louis's distillers from 1871 to 1875. There are many accounts from all parties involved in the ring. Many of them, including the federal cases and arrests that took place, claim that General Grant and many of his close colleagues were behind the ring for profit. Joyce said of Bristow, "Benjamin H. Bristow, of Kentucky, was the Brutus selected by political conspirators to stab and tumble down from his exalted station the President of the United States. A more willing individual could not be found to deal the blow or stab the man who lifted him from an obscure country lawyer in a border state, through the successive grades of district attorney and solicitor general, to the Secretaryship of the Treasury."

In the end the whiskey ring prosecution shrouded Grant in a questionable veil, cost the American people one million dollars, and caused the government losses of two million or more due to idle distilleries. The Whiskey Ring clearly demonstrates how important the whiskey commodity was. As the West was expanding, there was a movement that encouraged distribution, growth, and expansion of the market. Economic drivers like overproduction led to attempts at control and taxation. Control led to corruption, and lack of regulation allowed the same type of stock scandal with whiskey as was seen with Standard Oil and the railroads.

On the heels of the Whiskey Ring came the Distillers & Cattle Feeders Trust, also known as the Whiskey Trust. The Whiskey Trust involved a group of gentlemen who monopolized the whiskey business in Peoria, Illinois, in the 1880s. They wanted to control the whiskey and its dividends. Much of the whiskey being shipped to the frontier came from Peoria, where it had been distilled since the 1850s and was the whiskey capital during the late 1800s. It began when distiller Joseph Greenhut organized the "great Whiskey Trust." He modeled the trust after Rockefeller's Standard Oil Trust and created the Distillers & Cattle Feeders Trust. Rockefeller's trust of 1882 was created to allow Rockefeller and other Standard Oil stockholders to get around state laws prohibiting one company from owning stock in another. One of the ways the Whiskey Trust was able to hide the amount of whiskey they were producing from the Internal Revenue's gaugers was to use custom-made whiskey barrels. The *Herald* in Dallas, Texas, reported on this story, which broke in 1885. In the report they noted that some distillers in Peoria had been using whiskey barrels that were constructed with a thick stave that sat opposite the bung. The heads of the barrels were only half an inch thick versus the standard, three-quarters of an inch thick. The custom barrels could hold about one to one and one-half gallons more whiskey than the typical barrel. Some of the revenue gaugers were suspicious so they detained and inspected some of the barrels from large distilleries. The gaugers found the irregularity and discovered a man named Eads who was the cooper commissioned to create the custom barrels.[24]

In 1888 the *New York Tribune* reported that "eighty-one organizations formed the trust. . . . Of the total annual output of the Trust (40,000,000 gallons of spirits) about fifteen per cent was consumed as a beverage, 8,000,000 gallons was used in the arts, and the remainder in the manufactures and wine fortification." The Whiskey Trust fell apart in 1895 when the Illinois Supreme Court found that it had "usurped powers not conferred by its charter, that it was monopolistic in its operation and therefore was illegal."

Another market that undoubtedly had the biggest connection and profited the most from whiskey's influence included saloons, private clubs, brothels, and dance halls. As towns were created and settled by pioneers, saloons were often the first business to

Whiskey label of the Great Western Distilling Co., Peoria, Illinois, February 14, 1885. NEW YORK PUBLIC LIBRARY DIGITAL COLLECTIONS

open. Even Mark Twain noted this as he reached the head of the Mississippi River in Saint Paul, Minnesota:

> *It is a very wonderful town indeed, and is not finished yet. All the streets are obstructed with building material, and this is being compacted into houses as fast as possible, to make room for more—for other people are anxious to build, as soon as they can get the use of the streets to pile up their bricks and stuff in. How solemn and beautiful is the thought, that the earliest pioneer of civilization, the van-leader of civilization, is never the steamboat, never the railroad, never the newspaper, never the Sabbath-school, never the missionary—but always whiskey! Such is the case. Look history over; you will see. The missionary comes after the whiskey—I mean he arrives after the whiskey has arrived; next comes the poor immigrant, with axe and hoe and rifle; next, the trader; next, the miscellaneous rush; next, the gambler, the desperado, the highwayman, and all their kindred in sin of both sexes; and next, the smart chap who has bought up an old grant that covers all the land; this brings the lawyer tribe, the vigilance committee brings*

the undertaker. All these interests bring the newspaper; the newspaper starts up politics and a railroad; all hands turn to and build a church and a jail, and behold, civilization is established forever in the land. But whiskey, you see, was the van-leader in this beneficent work. It always is. It was like a foreigner—and excusable in a foreigner—to be ignorant of this great truth, and wander off into astronomy to borrow a symbol. But if he had been conversant with the facts, he would have said, "Westward the Jug of Empire takes its way."[25]

Chapter Four

Saloons: The Life, Breath, and Death in a Town

The saloon itself was a manifest of a male-dominated frontier. These establishments were the epicenter of most towns where men gathered to get their news, read newspapers and business journals, talk politics, and unwind. Sophisticated businessmen, farmers, hardworking miners, cowboys, and high-stakes gamblers were the saloon's customers, and many a deal was made over a whiskey cocktail, whether it was political, business, or social. In rural towns, saloons often served as the school or community center by day and a drinking and gambling mecca by night. As the towns boomed, so did the saloons, and their owners made rapid improvements to their businesses to keep them competitive. Drinking establishments spared no expense, coming up with new ways to entice customers through quality liquors and ever more elaborate interiors, as profits allowed.

The western saloon ranged from quickly erected dirt-floored tents illuminated with lanterns to elegant brick and wood establishments festooned with glimmering chandeliers, offering classical music, displaying expensive oil paintings, and importing elegant rugs to cover tiled floors. Furniture and glassware was ordered from San Francisco, the Midwest, and back East.

The Combination saloon was located in a mining town in nineteenth-century Utah. This photo shows the simplicity of the earliest phases of saloons, which were often tents or shacks evolving with the town's success.
UTAH STATE HISTORICAL SOCIETY

A popular artist of the day was Astley David Middleton Cooper, born in St. Louis, Missouri, in 1856. A. D. Cooper was an illustrator for *Frank Leslie's Illustrated Newspaper* and captured many of the West's images for the magazine. He became well known as a painter of the Old West and Indians. In 1879 he moved to San Francisco and became active with the local art association. His artwork was frequently found on saloon walls because—it was said—he would pay his bar bill with his paintings. On one occasion, when a saloon in San Francisco was being sold, one of his paintings was included in the list of contents. The ad read, "One large and elegant painting by A.D. Cooper, cost $2000 [$58,000 in today's money].[1] Elsewhere in the West, saloons featured other artists and subjects. Patrons of the Tombstone Headquarters saloon in Tombstone, Arizona Territory, stood at the wooden bar and gazed upon an eight-by-twelve-foot painting of a ship on canvas, which adorned the saloon's wall. Its owner, John J. Inwall, advertised his saloon as "a favorite place of resort for all those who are lovers of a delightful beverage." A nearby competitor was the elegant Alhambra saloon whose owners, Thomas Nichols and Joseph Mellgren, adorned their establishment with two splendid oil paintings of thoroughbred horses. Milton Joyce of the upscale Oriental Saloon in Tombstone hung *The Awakening*, an expensive oil painting, over his bar. Customers who stood at his bar could appreciate a very realistic nude woman awakening from sleep—the work was said to be worth one hundred dollars. In Nevada, artist C. B. McClellan painted a large portrait of the history of Virginia City, Nevada, that was displayed at a saloon in this lively mountainous town.

In the elaborately decorated fashionable saloons, keepers sold only the finest liquors, champagne, wine, and cigars that could be procured. Other saloons were pretty basic and consisted of a bar, spittoons, glassware, some gaming tables, and liquor. Most did not have tables or chairs in the main saloon area, but some did have a few card tables or reading tables in the back. Cocktails—rather than straight shots of whiskey—were the norm, despite what Hollywood often depicts. William F. "Buffalo Bill" Cody's favorite cocktail was the Stone Fence, and he often drank it at the Buckhorn Exchange saloon, which opened in Denver, Colorado, in 1893. It was owned and operated by Henry H. "Shorty Scout" Zietz, who was a lifelong friend of Buffalo Bill. Bill often visited his friend in Denver and drank his favorite libation. Today the Buckhorn honors Buffalo Bill with his favorite cocktail, but they call it the "Buffalo Bill."[2]

Mixologists prided themselves on knowing their customers and making sure they were completely satisfied with their saloon experience. In 1876 a Missouri newspaper ran an interview with a mixologist who claimed that most barkeepers could tell where a customer was from based on his drink order. He commented,

Buffalo Bill's Wild West Show elevated the status of the cowboy, and its tours around the world popularized the nostalgic West. LIBRARY OF CONGRESS

"Well, you see, sir, barkeepers can generally fix the nationality of the visitor by his drinks. Most all Americans that drink at all go for a gin or whisky cocktail in the morning. A French drinker either takes claret and ice, or if he is anyway hard on it some cognac or absinthe. . . . In this country, every State nearly has its own style of drinks. Of course, whisky is at the top of the heap; but then there are hundreds of brands and we try to suit all tastes. A New Yorker calls for rye, and a Pennsylvanian wants Monongahela; the North Carolina and Florida fellers stick up for corn whisky, and its nearly certain death to offer a Kentucky drinker anything but bourbon. . . . Missourians are great whisky-drinkers. They want their whisky straight and strong, and plenty of it."

When asked about not having what a customer wanted, the barkeep responded, "Suppose you don't happen to have the particular brand of whisky a gentleman calls for? Well, that's easily settled. There's mighty few bars where they keep both rye and bourbon, and between me and you there's not many drinkers who can tell the difference between 'em. Most bars keep two or more bottles of whisky (all drawn from the same barrel), and if a barkeeper understands his business he can make a customer believe he is drinking rye when he is actually drinking bourbon, or vice versa. Bad rye whisky with a dash of common bitters can be made to pass as corn whisky."[3]

Regardless of what a customer drank, saloon owners needed to supply their establishments with liquor and other goods. They ordered their liquor and other supplies from a variety of places, which often included agents in California. One of the bigger supply companies was Moore, Hunt & Co. in San Francisco, which in the 1880s was a main distributor of Kentucky whiskey to many frontier towns. They not only specialized in Kentucky whiskey but also sold Crown whiskey for eight dollars for one case. When ordering their whiskey, saloon owners chose from AA, A, B, or C brands and received discounts when they ordered in large quantities, such as cases or barrels. A barrel or half barrel of AA brand whiskey cost four dollars per gallon, while the same amount of C brand cost only three dollars. Some popular brands of US whiskey included Thistle Dew, Old Crow, Hermitage, Old Kentucky, Old Reserve, Overholt, Coronet, Log Cabin No. 1, O.K. Cutter, Chicken Cock and Rye, and Old Forrester. Imports included Dewar's Scotch, Jameson Irish Whiskey, and Canadian Club Whiskey.

Whiskey was the most popular spirituous beverage served in most saloons, but barkeeps also used it to make an assortment of cocktails, toddies, flips, and more. Three of the most famous mixologists operating in California during the nineteenth century were William "Cocktail" Boothby, Jerry Thomas, and Harry Johnson. Born in 1830, Jerry Thomas is considered to be the "Father of the Cocktail." Thomas tended bar at the Occidental Hotel in San Francisco in the 1860s, where one legend claims the martini's history starts. In 1862 "Professor" Thomas published the *Bartender's Companion*. He is also credited with creating the wildly popular Tom and Jerry cocktail while tending bar at the Occidental.

Companies like Moore, Hunt & Co. acted as wholesalers and distributors across the West. Circa 1890s. NATIONAL ARCHIVES

The mixologist was an admired role. Most were creative and entertaining, such as "Professor" Jerry Thomas, depicted here. He's showing off his famous flaming cocktail, the Blue Blazer. FABIO QUAGLIARINI

William T. "Cocktail" Boothby stood at the average height of 5'11" behind the bar, but he was tall in demand during the late nineteenth and early twentieth centuries. A large portion of his career was spent at the elegant Palace Hotel on Montgomery Street. It was at this establishment where he created his signature Boothby Cocktail. This California native came from a restaurant family so he likely learned his craft while working for his parents during the later part of the 1800s. He wrote his first bartender book called *The American Bartender* in 1891 and republished it after the turn of the century.

While Boothby was the head bartender at the Palace, he also filled in at the Fairmont Hotel and another downtown location. It was during this time when a patron of these establishments decided to stop drinking. This unnamed imbiber wandered into the Fairmont one afternoon where Boothby served him a cocktail, and he went on his way. He later patronized the downtown location where Boothby had started serving drinks. The man said to Boothby, "I've seen you somewhere before."

Boothby replied he didn't think so. The patron then asked, "Have you got a brother working at the Fairmont?"

Boothby told him he did not. The man muttered, "Most curious, more curious."

About an hour later, Boothby had stepped behind the bar at the Palace and that same patron walked up the mahogany board to order a beverage. Billy leaned over to take the man's order but rather than hearing a cocktail order, the man asked, "Have YOU got a brother at the Fairmont?"

Boothby replied, "No, sir, not I. What will you have?"

The paled-lipped patron moaned, "Not a thing! When I get as bad as this, it's time to quit. I'm through forever!"[4]

Harry Johnson also tended bar in San Francisco for a while and later wrote the 1882 *Bartenders' Manual*, which went into great detail as to how one should act and look behind the bar. It described how a bartender should address his customers, how to attain a job at a saloon, and how to set up a bar, and included hints on making drinks just right. Harry stated that in order for a bartender to make the best drink possible, he must take the customer's order and then ask if he liked it medium, stiff, or strong. He also needed to ascertain if the customer wanted a julep, a sour, or a toddy version of his drink. Harry concluded, "I can not avoid, very well, offering more remarks regarding the conduct and appearance of the bartender. . . . Bartenders should not, as some have done, have a tooth-pick in their mouth, clean their finger nails while on duty, smoke, spit on the floor, or have other disgusting habits."

Thomas, Johnson, Boothby, and other barkeepers kept cordials, bitters, and syrups on hand to make a variety of concoctions. Mixologists or bartenders of the time were often skilled and were jokingly referred to as pharmacists, professors, or chemists with a "medicine" chest. A variety of wines, champagne, sherry, port, brandy, and the glasses to match were also staples of a well-stocked saloon. Some of the most popular types of cordials included absinthe, vermouth, Bénédictine, Hennessey and Martell brandies, kirschwasser, anisette, mint cordial, applejack, schnapps, and crème de cacao. Mixers included mineral waters, soda water, carbonic acid, and cider. They also stocked a variety of syrups like pineapple, strawberry, raspberry, lemon, orange, and rock candy.

Men in suits, cowboys with hats, or weary miners who wanted to order a Rock and Rye or any other cocktail generally entered saloons through fourteen-foot double doors made of glass and wood, typical of the Victorian style. Unless they were housed in tents, businesses across the West had these doors. Many saloons also had a second set of interior doors behind the main entrance doors and these were sometimes swinging doors. Two sets of doors were good for business for various reasons: During the warmer months, the main doors could be opened for fresh air, but then dust would drift in. The swinging doors were also a way for passersby to hear the sounds of gambling, clinking glasses, cheers, and music to entice them in.

Harry Johnson's cocktail pouring trick. Mixologists of the day prided themselves on making good drinks but also often liked to impress their customers. Circa 1882. SHERRY MONAHAN

The traditional *saloon* was reserved for places where men drank, read newspapers, and conducted business and were managed by well-known and respected members of the community. Lower saloons and dance halls, on the other hand, were run by less-than-respected businessmen, pimps, rugged women, and madams. While they sold whiskey and made cocktails, they also provided "fancy" ladies for the men to dance with. Dancing was also a euphemism for something a little more engaging. Brothels also offered drinks and whiskey, but there was no doubt about what was going to happen when a patron visited one. The only women in most respectable saloons were singers and, on occasion, faro dealers, but this was the exception—not the rule. Toward the latter part of the nineteenth century, as social norms relaxed, some saloons did employ conservatively dressed waitresses to serve their customers. There were also the opera houses and theaters, which featured women entertainers like Sarah Bernhardt and Maude Adams. Some of the places they performed, like the Bird Cage Theatre in Tombstone, Arizona, were reserved for men attendees only. If there was a respectable theater in town, then the wives got to join their husbands to see those famous nineteenth-century actresses.

Because respectable women didn't dare enter a saloon, they found an alternative way to "get their drunk on" in the nineteenth century. The *Coffeyville Weekly Journal* in Kansas explained how women first began developing a thirst for, and later a dependency on, liquor. An investigation was conducted at an eastern prison for women where the prisoners were interviewed. It concluded that of the 204 inebriate women, most started by drinking beer or whiskey punches. As their need for a drink increased, 187 stated whiskey had become their favorite beverage.[5]

To satisfy their fondness for whiskey, women in the West often drank the cocktail bitters that mixologists used to flavor drinks or medicinal elixirs—bitters' main ingredient was whiskey. With their Victorian gowns swishing as they walked into the local mercantile store or called on their local chemist, they could respectfully pick up a bottle of bitters for their "health." Bitters companies knew this and used clever advertising to attract their non-saloon customers. The tonics were sold under the promise that they would ease common female illnesses, and they were also purported to ease or cure mental anguish, feverish lips, cracking pains, weak stomach, and scores of other nameless bodily suffering.

The B. W. Woodward Druggist and Manufacturing company called out the deception of these tonics. They were offering a non-whiskey tonic and claimed their competitors' tonics were nothing more than mislabeled whiskey. Their 1860s advertisement read: "A healthful, invigorating tonic, that should commend itself as a proper one to the medical profession, and be free from the objection of pandering to depraved appetite for whisky stimulants, under the specious name of 'tonic bitters,' has long been needed by the public." Directly under their ad was another one for Foster's Silurian Bitters, who claimed their bitters were the purest and best tonic stimulant ever brought to the market. Another competitor to B. W. Woodward was the maker of Leis' Dandelion Tonic, who also called out the tonic-drinking masses: "[It] is not a 'Whisky Bitters' or a 'Fancy Drink' that may lead the user to drunkenness and ruin, but it is a true and reliable medicine which has been used for the past fifteen years and has been prescribed by many leading physicians."[6, 7]

Not all of bitters' use as medicine was spurious or intentionally duplicitous. In some cases, whiskey was the only "anesthesia" available for illness or injury. Rheumatism, an inflammatory affliction that haunted many in the Old West, was said to be cured with whiskey. According to physician and author Dr. Chase's recipe, the afflicted pioneer should blend half an ounce of black cohosh root to one pint of the best rye whiskey. He recommended one to three teaspoons three times per day just before meals—at the very least, one might forget about the pain throughout the

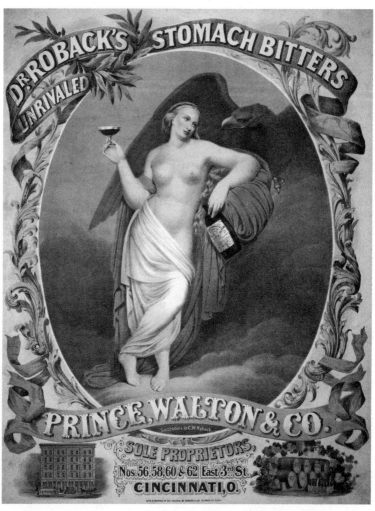

Hundreds of bitters were available to the pioneers and were widely promoted. Many ads targeted women and claimed medicinal properties and restorative abilities that were quite exaggerated. Circa 1866.
LIBRARY OF CONGRESS

day! A recipe for an old German medicine called "Life Tincture" appeared in another book and included whiskey, aloe, saffron, myrrh, nutmeg, and rhubarb.[8]

On the other hand, companies touted their cure-all medicines as nothing short of miracles in a bottle for any and all afflictions. In truth most consisted of opium or whiskey and some herbs. Some peddled their whiskey as medicine and didn't even try to hide it. George Simmond sold whiskey and trademark #7400 was filed on April 14, 1879, in San Francisco for his "Nabob," product. Simmond was a Kentucky native and made sure to use that to his advantage. His "Kentucky" Nabob Pure Bourbon Whiskey was a popular cure-all elixir in the 1880s. The ads read, "Medical Journals say that Simmond's Nabob Whiskey is a safe stimulant and very wholesome; can be safely used by all invalids; all who value their health should use Simmond's Nabob Whiskey; it is the purest and the best in the Market; being analyzed by the most eminent professors and pronounced by them free from adulteration, and recommended for medicinal and family use. Large bodies coming from everywhere for barrels and half barrels, shipped direct from the distillery in Kentucky. It has a very fine flavor, and is mild from old age; give it a trial, you then can judge for yourselves; sold by barrels, half barrels and cases by my agents on liberal terms. Endorsed by all leading physicians; kept by all druggists, grocers, and first class saloons. Beware of counterfeits; none genuine unless labeled with the signature and brand on the bottle." Ads like this one appeared in most local papers, and Simmond's had agents all over the West peddling his "cure all."

Even though whiskey elixirs were consumed in large quantities by men and women in the West, some found other uses for it. It was in 1865 Austin, Texas's *South and West* where a recipe was offered for horses with colic: "To one pint of whiskey add three tablespoons of gunpowder. Shake it ten minutes and then give to the horse. If in one hour he is not relieved, repeat the dose.[9]

These elixirs and cure-alls were sold at local pharmacies across the frontier, but the town of Columbus, Kansas, had enough and tried to stop the practice. In 1879 they had what amounted to a whiskey war, and all the druggists were fined one hundred dollars by the city for selling liquor without a license. They fought back by closing their businesses and posting signs on the doors that read, "Closed for ninety days; for particulars see city dads." A quick compromise was made when the druggists agreed to only sell their products for medicinal purposes. The *Girard Press* reported, "The trouble is that too many so-called drug stores in Kansas are nothing by dram-shops." The assault on the pharmacists didn't end. Another man, S. S. Belcher, of nearby Findlay City, was fined twenty-five dollars and court costs for selling intoxicating liquors without a license to one person and Home and Gin Bitters to numerous others.[10]

By the mid- to late 1800s, it was a known fact that the main ingredient in elixirs and bitters was rectified spirits. Many men and women had become alcoholics by simply drinking these cure-alls. The *Topeka Daily Capital* even published a lengthy story about the subject with the headline, "Puffing Whisky. What a Leading Physician Thinks of Doctors Giving Their Support to Alcoholic Advertisements." The story began, "I have been some-what mortified, as well as a little amused, at the publication lately in all the prominent newspapers of lengthy advertisement (con-taining testimonials from physicians) recommending a certain whisky as a cure, not only for almost all the maladies flesh is heir to, but especially as 'a cure for drunkenness.' . . . The other day a woman (visibly under alcoholic influences) called at my office to get my opinion as to the benefit to be derived from the use of this so-much advertised non-fusel-oil whiskey (meaning little or no alcohol). She got it, and it was that if she used a bottle or two more of the nasty poison she would become a drunkard." Much to her horror, he advised her that its main ingredient was whiskey and to stop taking it. He went on to state that during his last eight years as a doctor he had treated hundreds of inebriate patients who had succumbed to Rock and Rye.[11]

Humorist Robert Burdette was a staff writer for Iowa's *Burlington Hawkeye,* and his tongue-in-cheek commentary appeared in papers across the West. His apparent fondness for whiskey and temperance bitters was displayed in an 1887 *Des Moines Register* column where he noted, "I do not fly around and perspire because the government has decided to collect the whisky tax from the temperance bitters. I endorse the action of the government because I have always insisted that the temperance bitters contained the worst whisky, and should be reformed in this respect before they could be considered a proper drink for a prohibitionist. Moreover, it is unwholesome and wrong to mix greens and herbs with liquor."

One of the largest-selling brands of bitters was Hostetter's Stomach Bitters, and they were taken to task by a Kansas newspaper that claimed the bitters caused drunkenness. They wrote, "It is said the Hostetter, the compounder of that vile decoction known as 'Hostetter's Stomach Bitters,' has accumulated a fortune of eleven million. We would not become responsible for the wicked and murderous drunks his bitters have produced for ten times his earnings."[12]

Successful businessmen and -women all over the West turned a profit from whiskey, whether it was bitters, elixirs, or in a bottle. But the profits weren't limited to the actual product itself—other related business enterprises, such as pretty bottles used to display the golden elixir, also did well. The decanter business boomed when saloonkeepers used beautiful glass rather than whiskey bottles as a way to earn a healthier bottom line. They poured whiskey from decanters so their customers would not know exactly what product they were being served. This gave rise to those scenes in western films where the customer asks for "the good stuff." Many of the items like mixers and glassware were ordered from California and the largest cities back East. One firm in Chicago, Illinois, was Albert Pick & Company. They claimed they were the largest and oldest bar goods house in the United States. American Fork, Utah, bartender Hyrum Adamson ordered some of his supplies from Pick, which included cherries, a faucet, a brush, mops, and a beer scraper. Other items on hand in saloons were more for the customer's convenience. Some bartenders provided their sophisticated glove-wearing customers with a bar-spoon, since removing the gloves might prove difficult. The spoon was offered so the customer could take out some, or all, of the fruit that accompanied most fancy drinks of the time. Making a variety of fancy mixed drinks also required the saloonkeeper to have an array of drink glasses, including champagne, wine, whiskey, brandy snifter, pony, and cordial glasses.

Surprisingly, none of the recommended glasses in the old bartender books were called shot glasses. The closest thing to what's available today was called a whiskey glass, which looked like our modern shot glass and held one and one-half to two and one-half ounces. The first reference to the actual use of the term *shot glass* appeared in papers across the country in the early 1930s, and the words "shot glass" were always in quotation marks. In 1932 an Indiana judge heard a case about a *shot glass*, a term new to him. A restaurant owner was seen by police officers carrying three *shot glasses* of liquor. The judge listened as the defendant's attorney and a police officer discussed the matter. From that conversation he determined that a shot glass was the size of a drink of liquor—be it large or small. The defendant's attorney told the police officer that "shot glasses were very small and made of heavy glass." The police officer said, "No. My idea of a 'shot glass' is a glass that a man takes a 'shot' of liquor from in one drink."[13]

Regardless of what they were called, saloonkeepers often proudly stacked their shimmering crystal on the back bar. Sometimes having whiskey in a glittering decanter worked against them, such as was the case in Helena, Montana, where a patron couldn't help himself and absconded with a pretty decanter of whiskey. The *Helena Daily Herald* published a story in 1875 about a man they called Dead Beat, who was a former Union soldier in the Civil War. "While Dunk was engaged in dusting up the club room, this D.B. slipped the decanter into his pocket and himself out of the saloon. Dunk missed the decanter about as soon as he did the man, and started in pursuit. He captured the thief on Jackson street, conducted him back to the saloon and turned him over to Marks. Marks delivered a brief muscular sermon to the mis-guided ex-blue coat, gently conducted him to the street, and started him off in a very meditative mood." Isaac Marks's saloon was reported to be the oldest one in Helena that sold whiskey, and by 1889 it and thirty-five other saloons offered places of refreshment.[14, 15]

The science of drinking whiskey was explained in a western newspaper in the 1880s. Different varieties of alcohol proved to be an interesting subject for a man in San Francisco, California, in the early 1880s. The man, whose identity is unknown, conducted a scientific study on Canal Street, where he studied intoxicated men to determine what kind of alcohol they drank. A reporter approached the scientific man with a notebook and asked:

"You are an artist perhaps?"

"No, sir," said the man with the book. "My object is a scientific one. I am collecting facts designed to throw light upon the internal condition of the inebriate by noting his acts when intoxicated. Patients get too much of the lump treatment."

"*Then you are observing this man walk?*"

"*I am, sir. You know perhaps, that when certain parts of the brain are acted upon peculiar muscular movements may be perceived. By watching these we may learn something of the nature and extent of the alcohol influence, and give a fair guess of the number of years the drinker has spent seasoning himself. So, too, by analyzing a man's methods of locomotion we may ascertain the probable amount and even the kind of liquor he has been taking. Do men under the influence of champagne conduct themselves as they would if they had taken brandy?*"

The reporter asked, "Would you be willing to name some of the special effects of well-known liquors?"

The scientist claimed, "A gin drinker resisted the influence better after the first few drinks, and became more helpless after he had his quantum, more than the majority of the drinkers of spirits. Gin drinkers, however, recovered easily, although they often got sick.

"*The whiskey drinker got lively and excited and was often hardheaded and obstinate. His gyrations were most eccentric of all. The bracing power of whiskey was followed by unpleasant cerebral activity. Whiskey was popular because it took hold of a man. Imbibers rarely fell down because of the intricacy of their method of walking. Common whiskey was a bad drink because of the large amount of amylic poison it contained. Those who liked Irish whiskey took a sort of 'cow-path' route. Consumers of this alcohol tended to fall straight forward, but sometimes they just fell in a heap. Scotch whiskey connoisseurs developed an easy, rolling, liberal gait, and drinkers of this libation are subject to various peculiarities.*

"*St. Croix rum drinkers did not talk loudly, nor sway as much as the whiskey drinker did. A rum drinker kept more clearheaded, but was prone to get weak in the knees. When they walked, they took a few straight steps, and they suddenly veered sidewise." According to the scientist, all these theories were null and void if the consumer had mixed his choice of beverage. "In applejack, the victim almost always fell upon his back. In walking, he raised his feet as if trying to climb stairs. Drinkers of applejack seemed to become intoxicated rather quickly, [it] acted as a sleeping aid, and was more potent than Rye whiskey." The scientist said of applejack, "Its power of raising the imagination to a high degree of foolishness is well known."*

The curious reporter asked one final question, "What had the man we just saw been drinking?"

The scientist replied, "He had, no doubt, been mixing the alcohol with malt. We will inquire." The two entered the saloon that the man had just departed from and asked the bartender.

"That man," exclaimed the saloonkeeper on being questioned, "the one you saw go out? Bless your soul sir, that's old Uncle Ben. He never misses his daily intoxication. He has discovered the quickest and most economical way of getting off. First, he calls for the biggest quantity of Scotch whiskey we will sell for fifteen cents; then he takes a schooner of beer, and in five minutes it's settled."[16]

A unique type of whiskey was being touted in Fort Scott, Kansas. The town had started as a military post to protect emigrants heading west, but eventually the post was closed and a town emerged. In 1886 it was thriving and even had its own brand of whiskey—well, sort of. The *Fort Scott Weekly Monitor* published a tongue-in-cheek story about "Horse Thief" whiskey. It reported, "Colonel Isaac Stadden missed his horse and wagon Tuesday night. Joe Mitchell, (the same that advertised the lost marriage license,) managed to get some whiskey—a peculiar kind of whiskey—that someone in Fort Scott is evidently furnishing, that makes a man thinks after he drinks it, that every horse he sees belongs to him. Joe Mitchell got some of this whiskey and drank it, and seeing Col. Stadden's horse hitched at Dr. Heplar's office, straightway took him, and did not discover his mistake until he got sober, which took twenty-four hours. We have often heard of 'rot-gut whiskey,' and 'bug juice,' '40-rod' whiskey, 'tarantula juice,' etc. We suppose that this kind that Mitchell got hold of was horse whiskey. We insist that the vendor of this thief making whiskey should be found out and punished. No man should be allowed to sell whiskey that makes men steal. The old kind in the days before prohibition was bad enough, but the man who will sell larcenous whiskey ought to be punished worse than the horse thief." Maybe the horse thief whiskey sufferer should have paid attention to the Duffy's Malt Whiskey ad that appeared the week before his incident. Duffy's large advertisement appeared in the *Weekly Monitor* to entice residents to buy its brand. The ad read, "Duffy's Pure Malt Whisky. What Is It. It is a superior brand of pure whiskey, its chief merit being that it is distilled by a secret process discovered by us in 1860, whereby every trace of fusel oil and other injurious substances are eliminated. It is the only whiskey of its kind manufactured in the world and is the only absolutely pure whiskey on the market. While as a whiskey and for every purpose to which whiskey is put, either as a medicine or drink, it is unequaled by any other whiskey.... Another peculiar feature of it is that it is the only whiskey that will stay on the stomach of invalids and debilitated persons." The ad went on for another hundred words or so explaining why its brand was the only brand to buy. In the end, it claimed, "Another thing we would impress upon our friends is not to be deceived.... It is under this guise that several unscrupulous manufactures are trying to reap the benefits from our name and prestige."[17, 18]

The high times for whiskey production and drinking were great for those who enjoyed a fine sipping spirit, but the men and women who felt drinking was the ruin of the world would not be silent. By 1889 many cities and states had enacted prohibition

Miraculous Cure of Pneumonia

Miss Susie John Cotton, of Jackson, Tenn., Relieved From Her Intense Pain After She Had Taken the Very First Dose of Duffy's Pure Malt Whiskey.

MISS SUSIE JOHN COTTON.

To thoroughly appreciate the extraordinary healing powers of Duffy's Pure Malt Whiskey, read what Miss Cotton says in her letter:

"Very recently I was taken ill on a train with what proved to be pneumonia; so seriously ill as to attract the attention of my fellow passengers, among whom was the Rev. A. N. Stephens, D. D., of Oakland, Tenn.

"At the next station he procured me a bottle of Duffy's Malt Whiskey, and I am glad to say that the very first dose brought comfort and alleviation from my intense pain. I continued to take the medicine and rapidly recovered my former good health. I think the cure in my case is well nigh a miracle."—MISS S. J. COTTON, Jackson, Tenn., July 14, 1905.

Duffy's Pure Malt Whiskey

For more than fifty years Duffy's Pure Malt Whiskey has been prescribed by doctors and used in over two thousand leading hospitals as the greatest tonic-stimulant and health-builder known to medical science. Duffy's Pure Malt Whiskey cures coughs, colds, consumption, grip, bronchitis and pneumonia. It stimulates and enriches the blood, aids digestion, builds up the nerve tissue, tones up the heart and fortifies the system against disease germs. It prolongs life, keeps the old young and the young strong. Duffy's Pure Malt Whiskey contains no fusel oil and is the only whiskey recognized by the Government as a medicine. This is a guarantee.

CAUTION—Be careful to get the genuine when you ask for Duffy's Pure Malt Whiskey. Sold in sealed bottles only; never in bulk. Look for the trade-mark, the "Old Chemist," on the label, and be sure the seal on the bottle is unbroken. All reliable druggists and grocers, or direct, $1.00 a bottle. Advice and medical booklet free. Duffy Malt Whiskey Co., Rochester, N. Y.

Whiskey was advertised for many years as medicine, often claiming it cured multiple illnesses, before the FDA began regulating it in 1906. SALT LAKE TELEGRAM, 1905

laws against drinking. Many of them had a hard time enforcing the laws, as was the case with some locales in northern Iowa. Reverend J. A. Chamberlain visited the area to observe if and how the prohibition movement was working. He commented on "how I saw men and women drunk, how I was disturbed by rows at early cock-crowing, how I saw sugar by the barrel, and all this. But on the other hand, I could tell you of cities where I could find no trace of the liquor traffic, where I hunted in vain for a place to 'irrigate.' I could tell you of visiting one city about half the size of Grand Forks [North Dakota], and searched for six days. Was at last told where I could get a drink of whisky. And where was it? A certain scavenger had by some turn around obtained a quantity of liquor, and in the rounds of his odoriferous business he carried also a flask of whiskey out of which men could drink on the payment of fifteen cents. My conclusion was simply this, that the whole matter was with the people. The law was not a force. If the people desired they had no saloon. If indifferent to the law, they violated it."[19]

Cities and towns often reacted to the very vocal temperance followers, but also felt the pressure of businesses and imbibers. By the 1890s, regional prohibition laws had relaxed in many locales, and cities like St. Louis, Missouri, became major distributors of Kentucky and Tennessee whiskey. In 1892 the *Pen and Sunlight Sketches of St. Louis* was published, and it noted that St. Louis had long enjoyed the reputation of being one of the largest and best whiskey markets in the world. They also stated that St. Louis had many of the largest liquor houses in the United States. The long-established St. Louis firm of S. J. Lang & Sons was prominently written about in that same sketchbook. It noted, "The house of S. J. Lang & Sons, proprietors of the Kentucky Prince Distillery and dealers in superior wines and liquors, is one of special prominence in St. Louis. The business was established in 1867 by Mr. S. J. Lang at Rolla, Mo., being confined to the wholesale liquor business at that time, and the sons of Mr. Lang were admitted to the firm and the present style formed. The firm now consists of the following: Mr. S. J. Lang, the founder, and his sons, A. J. Lang and Sig. J. Lang. The Kentucky Prince Distillery is located in Anderson County, Kentucky, and the special brands of fine whiskies distilled by this house are Kentucky Prince, Bell Rose, Madison, Blue Grass Pride, Kentucky Queen, 1876 Red Ribbon, Robert E. Lee, and Cherokee Club. This house also has the sole agency for the Monarch Mills, and makes a specialty of the famous Red Ribbon whisky."

While St. Louis was a major whiskey player, California merchants were also big shippers of whiskey to locations all over the West. The April 1892 issue of the *Pacific Wine and Spirit Review* noted, "While it is true that many dealers are complaining of dull times, it is equally true that they are laying in good stocks in anticipation of the better times to come. The spring trade is rather late, but that it will be active, the general prosperous condition of the coast and the almost assured good crops of 1892 would seem to warrant. The replacement of the compounded goods by straights and blends goes steadily on and the receipts of whisky from the East this year bid fair to equal if not to exceed those of spirits and alcohol." They noted that receipts for American whiskey in March alone included 40 cases and 440 barrels delivered to San Francisco by sea from Atlantic ports. They received 46 cases and 1,950 barrels by overland rail. In addition, they received 30 cases of foreign whiskeys. They also exported 416 cases and 850 gallons of whiskey, with a value of $4,275 in the month of March.[20]

Popular 1890s American Whiskeys

The prices are per gallon as sold by San Francisco merchants:

Our Favorite OK $2.75 to $3.50
Paul Jones $2.25 to $2.50

Old Crown $1.75 to $2.00
Carlisle, bottled in cases $9.50
Nonpareil $2.50 to $5.00
Blue Grass, Spring '83 $2.75
OK Extra $3.50 to $6.00
Golden Pearl $2.25
OK Goldwater $4.00
Union Club 100 proof $2.25
Gold Medal 100 proof $2.50
Phoenix Old Bourbon A1 $2.75
Old Rip Van Winkle $2.50
Nevilles Old Bourbon $1.50
O.K. Old Stock $5.00

Source: *Pacific Wine & Spirits Review*, April 1892

Whiskey shipments, whether by rail, freight, or ship, were in danger of being stolen, damaged, or lost as they made their way to consumers across the frontier. Quite a few ships with whiskey in their cargo holds were lost to the turbulent rivers in the West from the early to mid-1800s. In the 1890s dreams of buried liquid gold and a quest to recover it became an obsession for many treasure seekers. In 1893 a Kansas newspaper reported on buried whiskey and the recovery efforts: "The oldest wreck of which there is now any knowledge . . . is of the Spanish boat that was sunk at the mouth of the River Des Peres in south St. Louis. It is also said, by the way, that the Spanish vessel had on board a goodly stock of liquors. . . . Just think how far a barrel of goods made 'in the early years' and thus preserved would go in this time of quickly-aged whiskies!" According to the article, the oldest wreck of which the newspaper had firsthand knowledge, was a government steamer that sank in the Missouri River in the early 1830s at Arrow Rock Island near Boonville. Its cargo included gold and whiskey, and it was rumored that some of the whiskey had been privately recovered. The *Arabia*, a side-wheel steamboat, was another ship that went down in 1856 below Parkville, also in the Missouri River. Her journey began on August 1, 1856, at St. Louis and was bound for Omaha, Nebraska, and Council Bluffs, Iowa. She was loaded with pork, Wedgewood queens-ware, and two hundred to six hundred barrels of high-quality whiskey. Her captain was Dan Able, who guided her like he had done before. This journey was no different until August 20 when he reached Parkville, Missouri. As he tried to maneuver the boat to the landing, the hull was pierced when it was snagged by sunken trees and began taking on water. Newspaper reports claim the captain lost his head and panicked and swung the boat into the stream of the river. After the ship drifted downstream, the engines could not hold against the current and the boat hit the opposite bank. Even though the boat didn't completely sink, the whiskey and queens-ware were completely underwater in the boat's hold. Rumors of whiskey rescued from the *Arabia* swirled, and the *Salina Daily Republican* smirked, "If it is so, the finders must have lost their heads sampling the quality of goods, and thus forgot the lay of the river at the lucky point." Not long after the *Arabia* was sunk, the *Ogden*, captained by Jim Bissell, suffered the same fate. It sank a few miles above Jefferson City and was thought to be the one with the best hope of recovery. Two years after the *Ogden* went down, the *Twilight* was sunk.[21]

The *Twilight*'s story began on a foggy August morning in 1865 when the side-wheel steamboat was making her way up the Missouri to Kansas City. Fog made it difficult to navigate, and the boat struck the shore in a bend in the river near Camden. The passengers and crew were all removed to safety, but the cargo could not be salvaged. It was a terrible loss for the cargo owners, because there were three hundred gallons of Monongahela rye whiskey in the hold. The owners of the ship were going to net fifty thousand dollars for its efforts to deliver the whiskey, wine, barrels of castor and linseed oil, and canned goods. The ship eventually sank into the muddy waters and sat nearly untouched for thirty years. A newspaper report from 1896 stated, "It was expected that if the wreck should be found enormous profits would be made from the whisky, providing it was in good condition. It was Monongahela rye, old fashioned copper distilled, made in the days when pure Whisky was the rule." In February 1896 the Kansas City Wrecking Company was formed of capitalists and businessmen. They obtained permission from the government to seek the liquid treasure. They were fortunate because of the amount of time that had elapsed, meaning they didn't have to seek the original owner's permission. After months of working on getting to the cargo, they descended into the hold of the *Twilight*. They first found some boxes of Old London Gin, which was said to be delicious, but they were there for the whiskey. In the beginning, they were only able to salvage some of the three hundred barrels, but they eventually got it all. A newspaper report captured the excitement over the aged whiskey:

> *The 300 barrels of whisky in the hold have not all been uncovered, but some of them have, and the barrels are in a perfect state of preservation. One of them was tapped, and the whisky was found to be even better than the gin. A glass of it, which was poured out before a company of men in the Kansas City Club, filled the entire floor with its aroma. It was thick and oily, almost of the consistency of New Orleans molasses, and after the glass was emptied it clung to the sides as sirup would. Whisky connoisseurs who have sampled it say that it exceeds anything in the whisky line that they have ever dreamed of.*

Removal of the barrels didn't happen for two weeks or more, because the wrecking company wanted the government officials to see it and make sure it was tax free. They argued that the taxes were paid at the distillery where the stuff was made more than thirty years ago. There was also a rumor that whiskey was found in the purser's cabin, which contained a safe with a large sum of money that was being carried from St. Louis to upriver merchants and army posts.

The newspaper article continued,

> *The money question, however, is forgotten for the present in the joy of the wreckers at the finding of the whisky and gin. This city and the surrounding country have gone wild over the find. One of the wreckers ventured the opinion that no crops would be grown in the vicinity till the excitement had died out. Soon after the whisky was found more than 500 farmers had gathered about the caisson watching the operations. In half the saloons in Kansas City "Twilight" whisky is being sold, though not a drop of the genuine article has been placed on sale. Those who have sampled the alleged "Twilight" whisky say it is more like "torchlight" whisky. Speculation is rife as to what will be the profits of the wreckers. Experienced whisky dealers say that it will sell readily for at least $400 a barrel.*[22]

A year after the *Twilight*'s whiskey was recovered, so was the *Arabia*'s. It was December 7, 1897, when her cargo hold was accessed, and while they hadn't yet removed the whiskey, they were working on a plan. If they couldn't remove the barrels, then they were going to siphon the whiskey out of what they called a "whiskey mine." A report from the time stated, "Previous to the discovery made yesterday the location of the Arabia has been but conjecture and the magnificent find will be hailed with delight, especially by those desirous of knowing the exact condition of the 600 barrels of forty-year-old 'stuff' that is said to have been buried in sand since 1856. . . . In case the barrels cannot be removed, the liquor is to be tapped into kegs and placed in hogsheads. This whiskey is said to have been of superior quality, and with its 41 years of age, is expected to be the finest ever placed on the American market."[23]

While the residents of Missouri were enjoying their newly recovered whiskey, the residents of Elk Point, South Dakota, were anticipating theirs. Their whiskey was coming from the sunken ship named the *Eldora*. Her journey began on April 1, 1866, and she was en route from St. Louis to Fort Benton, Montana. The *Eldora* carried 226 tons of freight including 116 barrels of whiskey. On May 21 the ship caught on fire and she was run ashore to be sunk with the hope of saving the cargo. No one was able to recover the cargo until 1896 when E. E. Wenner and his partner Fred Rush made the effort. The paper noted, "If the whisky is there Messrs. Wenner & Rush will make a small fortune. They have already had a number of offers of $10 a gallon for the stuff."[24]

Despite the excitement of aged whiskey in sunken ships, distilleries were still hard at work making their own new whiskey to sell. The Shawhan and Holladay distilleries had merged in 1900, and they kept the name Shawhan but operated at the location of Holladay's in Weston, Missouri. Their tagline was, "It Keeps on Tasting Good." The *Kansas City Star* reported, "Shawhan is the only distillery of any note west of the Mississippi River making a large amount of fine whiskey. West of the Mississippi River more consumers use SHAWHAN whiskey than any other brand. It has grown in favor so rapidly as to necessitate an increased production every year." They also noted that the Missouri Valley produced the best grains for distilling, and Shawhan had the benefit of local limestone springs to make their product superior.[25]

Other Missouri distillers were doing well, and by 1905 J. Rieger & Co. had become one of the largest whiskey distillers in Kansas City. The company began in 1887 and quickly grew, producing their private label called Monogram, which was sold by the quart for their eight- and ten-year-old rye whiskies.

The moral landscape of the West changed as it evolved from male-dominated, whiskey-drinking tent towns to sophisticated saloon-sipping brick cities. This movement took place as the wives, mothers, and children of those men living on the frontier arrived.

Shawhan Distillery, circa 1900. J. RIEGER DISTILLERY

The original J. Rieger & Co. distillery that was located in the West Bottoms
neighborhood of Kansas City, directly across from the Livestock Exchange
building. Circa 1900. J. RIEGER DISTILLERY

In the early 1900s J. Rieger & Co. offered a free quart of Crown black-berry brandy, a corkscrew, and a gold-rimmed glass with their motto, "O! So Good," with every purchase. Later they swapped out the blackberry and began offering two free sample bottles of whiskey with the glass and corkscrew. In their ad they claimed, "Over 250,000 customers have proven that our whiskey is far the best ever distilled. For smoothness and mel-lowness of flavor it cannot be equaled. Money refunded if whiskey is not perfectly satisfactory. Order today." This is one of the original bottles and whiskey glasses that J. Rieger offered as a promotional item in the 1800s.
J. RIEGER DISTILLERY

Women came to town and insisted on churches, schools, social clubs, and a more refined way of living—in other words, society. Not to say that some places like Denver, Colorado, or Portland, Oregon, didn't have any of these things before women arrived, but the whole social realm of living in the West changed dramatically. Over time, as whiskey consumption and drunkenness increased, women began campaigning across America to ban alcohol. The American West's favorite libation was about to be dealt a lethal blow.

Put Your Money Where Your Mouth Is

Not unlike today, people drank on a dare or a bet. Denver resident William Schroeder was one of those 19th century men who drank ten whisky cocktails in five minutes to win a wager. While he may have won his bet, he spent his winnings to save his life when he had his stomach pumped with a galvanic battery.

Source: *Daily Nonpareil* (Council Bluffs, Iowa), December 15, 1882

The Women's Christian Temperance Union was created in the 1870s as more whiskey was being consumed and alcoholism became more prevalent. They gained support when they formed an allegiance with suffragettes Susan B. Anthony, Elizabeth Cady Stanton, and other women battling for temperance and prohibition. Wives had grown tired of their husbands spending time in saloons and coming home drunk on whiskey cocktails. It may have been okay for single men or men whose wives were back East to get drunk in a saloon, but it was not once the men married or their wives joined them in the West. As the nineteenth century drew to a close, alcoholism among women had become a problem as well.

Whiskey Consumption Stats

In 1889 whiskey, by far, was the most consumed distilled spirit in America. A US report shared these numbers for proof gallons that had been consumed that year:

Whiskey: 879,282
Brandy: 100,482

Rum: 87,378
Gin: 84,937

Source: *Annual Report of the Commissioner of Labor*, 1898

In 1889 the Women's Christian Temperance Union went on a crusade over Rock and Rye tonics and candy drops. They were outraged that children were getting drunk on Rock and Rye

Women's holy war cartoon shows a crusader destroying barrels of whiskey, gin, etc. Circa 1874. LIBRARY OF CONGRESS

products that were advertised as healing medicine. They began a movement to have all the candy banned. "We have gone to many of the small retail candy dealers lately and requested them to stop the sale of rock-and-rye candy. Many of them complied with the request, but it is still manufactured and sold in large quantities. Even small bottles of rock and rye are also vended. We certainly do object to this feature of the candy business. Why, all our children will become premature drunkards if it shall be allowed to continue. When once they get in the habit of purchasing such articles at candy stores, they will then take a nip on the sly in some secluded beer saloon." They implored the makers to stop using whiskey and other alcohol to make their medicine, or be required to have a liquor license. They didn't buy into the manufacturer's comments that there was no basis for their concern. They argued, "The manufacturers of cordials and rock-and-rye candy claim that such action upon the part of the temperance ladies is a species of fanaticism. 'Why, if a child could eat ten pounds of rock-and-rye candy,' said a well-known confectioner of this city yesterday, 'it would not make him or her intoxicated in the least. I admit that there is some little of intoxicating spirits in such candy, but it is very small. I do not suppose there is one-quarter of a thimbleful of whisky in twenty-five rock-and-rye drops. These people cannot do any harm to us, and all their talk is mere twaddle.'" It's understandable that the makers of these candies and elixirs didn't want anyone to know how much whiskey was in their products, so distilleries labeled products as "medicinal" to avoid paying the higher taxes that were placed on liquor. Medicine had a tax, but it was less. They also wanted to dodge arguments like the ones the Women's Christian Temperance Union was making.[26]

Alcohol abuse was so prevalent by the late 1800s that doctors came up with the latest and greatest cure-alls for alcoholism. While most did not include whiskey, they contained cocaine and other similar elements! Dr. Leslie Keeley was a Dwight, Illinois, resident born of Irish parents. He had practiced various methods to cure people of alcohol addiction, but it wasn't until 1887 when he created the Double Chloride of Gold treatment. He began opening franchises of the Keeley Institute across the country, including one in Great Falls, Montana. Patients, usually of affluence because of the cost, would arrive at the facility and be given instructions. They had to give up their alcohol or drug, receive four injections over a three-week period, and stay at a nearby hotel. By 1892 Keeley claimed that he cured over sixty thousand addicted souls with a 95 percent cure rate. The cost was a mere thirty dollars per week for treatments only and did not include hotel costs. Butte, Montana, attorney George Haldorn recalled his experience with the treatment: "I didn't have the slightest idea that I would be cured. . . . In my mind, as in the minds of others, was just one predominating idea. That was, that there might be a possibility of my getting cured and I wanted to get all the whisky in me I could while I had the chance. For about four days I was as lively a drunk as the winds of Cheyenne ever blew." After his whiskey binge he took his shots at 8:30 a.m., noon, and 4:00 and 7:00 p.m. for twenty-two days for a total of eighty-six injections. He claimed he lost the taste for whiskey and tobacco and never felt better. Despite a few deaths directly after treatment, Keeley claimed there were no cases on record where death could be traced to his "gold" treatment. A doctor in San Francisco, not quite as prolific as Keeley, proposed to inoculate children to prevent adult alcoholism. He tested his theory with partial success by injecting some children with the blood of a drunken horse.

Pint-size Imbibers

Whiskey drinking wasn't limited to unshaven miners or clean-cut businessmen in top hats. Imbibing was common practice across America, but most assume adults were doing the drinking. Thinking back to the mid-nineteenth century, there were no real age-limit drinking laws, but there were certain society standards.

An English gentleman named Sir Henry Veel Huntley visited the San Francisco area in 1852 and noted, "These hotels are bad schools for children; some now running wild, not more than six or seven years of age, are already very conversant with the cigar, and with the oaths so frequently used by the American in common parlance. Two of these children came into the 'gentlemen's parlour' last evening, late, each bringing a glass of whiskey toddy, smoking each a cigar, and drawing their chairs to the stove, threw their feet upon it in the most approved fashion."[27]

While Montana resident Mr. W. Sampson wasn't a drunk in need of Keeley's treatment, he should have visited a doctor rather than take advice from a friend. He was brought before Judge Kennedy's court in Anaconda for disturbing the peace. Sampson, who had been sober for two years, had gotten drunk trying to cure himself from "the grip." It seems a friend of his advised that there was nothing better for the grip than Rock and Rye. Sampson trusted his friend and headed to the store and got himself a bottle. He felt so good after consuming the first bottle that he proceeded to get a second. In the midst of his second bottle, Sampson "kicked up quite a fuss" and was arrested. When he was brought before Judge Kennedy the court asked him if he could restrain himself and not go back to drinking. He told the judge he wasn't sure, so the judge said, "Wouldn't it be better for you if you went to jail for 30 days, so as to give you an opportunity to thoroughly sober up again?"

Sampson replied, "I haven't the slightest objection in the world."[28]

Inebriates like Sampson were prime examples of why the women's temperance movement was gaining support. In 1894 the Census Bureau reported there were 257 cities in America, 15,300,000 residents in those cities, and 61,000 saloons, equaling one saloon for every sixty families. The temperance movement found those numbers alarming, and they were reported and presented by the *National Baptist World* paper in Kansas City, Kansas.

In 1905 saloonkeepers were no longer making up large batches of Rock and Rye for their customers because the Internal Revenue Division started charging them twenty-five dollars per year to sell "ready-made" libations. In the West, inspectors made their way around frontier saloons to make sure the new law was being followed. When they arrived in Boise, Idaho, they found that several saloon owners were in violation; they all claimed that they were unaware of the new law. It appears the inspectors chose to make the proprietor of the Olympic saloon an example and arrested him. He quickly filed an affidavit stating that he was ignorant of the law. The *Idaho Daily Statesman* reported, "Inspectors have discovered that it has long been the practice of several local liquor dealers to mix rock candy and rye whisky into a decoction technically known as 'Rock and Rye,' a most fabulous drink, as well as a valuable remedy for la grippe." They noted that it was illegal for any saloon to mix up large quantities and keep it on hand unless they paid their fee.[29]

The *Salt Lake Telegram* reported about the same thing: "Bartenders will no longer mix up large amounts of 'rock and rye' so it may be ready when the customer calls for it. If you feel that your cold needs a little of that particular stimulant, the polite bartender will place a glass on the bar, pour in a little piece of the 'rock' and you may pour in the 'rye' yourself. Nor will Mr. Bartender mix up any other kind of drink and keep it in stock and ready for quick service."[30]

Because of tax evasion on the part of the elixir makers and the controversy surrounding the ingredients in them, as well as in other adulterated foods and whiskeys, the federal government was about to control the authenticity of the industry. Labeling of products was regulated by the federal government under the Pure Food and Drug Act of 1906. At first the act was interpreted to require that rectified products could not use the word *whiskey* without a modifier such as *imitation, compounded,* or *blended*. Rectifiers were to be barred from using the term *bourbon*, making age claims, or duplicating the labels of famous brands such as Old Crow and Old Grand-Dad, all of which were common practices. The rectifiers were understandably appalled by this interpretation and attacked the bourbon interests for selling dangerous, unwholesome fusel oil whiskey. Fusel oil is generally a mixture of several higher-carbon alcohols that occur in small percentages during fermentation, add considerable flavor, and are a key component of making a great whiskey. Most folks didn't know that, so rectifiers took advantage by making the claim that it was a good thing *not* to have fusel oils and promoting their whiskey as such. Lengthy and rancorous hearings were held in the US Congress, where whiskey quality was by no means an abstract concept. As the battle lines were being drawn, the Women's Christian Temperance Union supported the straight whiskey side, stating it was the lesser of two evils. This act also was the demise of the snake oil salesmen who sold bitters and tonics that contained many unknown ingredients.

Whiskey trading cards like this 1870 one for Old Crow were very popular across the frontier. This one was very risqué for its time. LIBRARY OF CONGRESS

This Whiskey War raged until 1909, when President William Howard Taft issued the Taft Decision. Now, rectified goods would be called blended whiskey and the traditional product would be called straight whiskey, but both had an equal right to the name whiskey. Later, even more precise definitions were written for bourbon, rye, and other types. Until the industry was regulated, most of the whiskey consumed on the frontier was as wild and untamed as the landscape and pioneers themselves.

Whiskey, whether it was pure-distilled, rectified, or rotgut, was the choice of pioneers, emigrants, saloonkeepers, and many others who called the West home. Whiskey was also the fuel that propelled businesses such as saloons, barrel makers, and many others who helped the West grow and prosper.

CHAPTER FIVE

Calls of Eureka and Giddy-Up: The Mining and Cattle Influence

AROUND THE SAME TIME BRIGHAM YOUNG STARTED DISTILLING his Valley Tan whiskey in what is now Utah, a woodsman named Isaac Graham arrived in California and settled near the mission of Santa Cruz, where he made his own wheat whiskey. A contemporary of Graham's, Zephryin Englehardt would later write, "Much ado was made about an American backwoodsman named Isaac Graham, who with others of his kind had found his way to California, and had settled down near Branciforte opposite Mission Santa Cruz. The distilling of whisky from wheat seemed to be his chief occupation. His disorderly associates organized a company of riflemen and made him their captain."[1]

The region now known as the state of California—claimed by Spain and then Mexico and also settled and explored by Russian fur traders—was seeing some settlement by other Europeans but was still largely unsettled until James W. Marshall, who was working to build a mill on the American River near the settlement of Coloma, saw something gold and shimmering in the water. The New Jersey native was working for entrepreneur John Sutter, when he appeared, rain-soaked, at Sutter's home later that day with a small item wrapped in a cloth. When Sutter unfolded the cloth and gazed upon the golden nuggets found on his land, he set in motion a chain of events that are well known to history.

Sutter, understandably, did not want the news about this discovery shared, but it's quite possible that whiskey was the reason the story was leaked. A Swiss teamster who had a penchant for whiskey seems to have foiled Sutter's plan. Sutter was in need of supplies and sent the trusted teamster to Coloma to get them. On the way there the teamster met up with some men who offered him gold dust and claimed they knew where to find more. After he got his supplies for Sutter, the teamster felt he deserved a much-needed drink and stopped at a mercantile store called Smith & Brannan's that sold goods and whiskey to make his purchase. Hubert Howe Bancroft recalled this teamster,

> *Often he tried at Smith and Brannan's store to quench his thirst from the whiskey barrel, and pay for the same with promises. On this occasion, he presented at the counter a bold front and demanded a bottle of the delectable, at the same time laying down the dust. "What is that?" asked Smith.*
>
> *"Gold," was the reply. Smith thought the fellow was quizzing him; nevertheless, he spoke of it to Sutter, who finally acknowledged the fact. About the same time . . . Sutter's schooner went down the river, carrying specimens of the new discovery. . . . Smith, store-keeper at the fort, sent word of it to his partner [Brannan].*[2]

Marshall made his discovery in January 1848; within four short years the boom would be over, leaving Sutter destitute. Millions were made and lost in a short time. Some men built empires on mining or selling goods and services to miners. Others went bust and turned to farming and labor in California, and some moved to other western locations. Even John Sutter, on whose land the gold was discovered, ended up dying in a cheap boardinghouse.[3]

During the height of the rush, however, places like Hangtown (now Placerville) and Coloma were teeming with thousands of men bent over the cold water of the American River and its many branches. They toiled hard during the day sluicing and swirling in search of nuggets and gold dust in El Dorado. But at night, they spent what they found on gambling and drinking. Gold was the main currency—either in nuggets or dust sacks. Bancroft recalled of the miners, "If hot, they drank to get cool, if cold, to get warm, if wet, to get dry—and some were always dry—to keep out the wet."[4]

Because the mine sites were remote, merchants could—and did—charge exorbitant prices for everything. In January 1848 the cost of flour was $4 per hundredweight (two hundred pounds) and beef was $2 per hundredweight. By December of that year, flour cost $27 and beef $20. Whiskey was selling at $40 per barrel in 1848. At the height of the rush, most stores charged $1 per pound for most items, but some places charged as much as $5 per pound. Eggs were rare and sold anywhere from $1 to $8 apiece. On average, miners yielded anywhere from $1 to $128 worth of gold and dust per day. Gold was selling between $12 and $16 per ounce in 1848. Rates for provisions soared to over four hundred times their value.[5]

A gold rush pioneer from Panama recalled his 1849 arrival: "At the time of our arrival, on the 15th of August, at the 'Embarcadero,' as Sacramento was then called, there was not a frame building in the town, except a small one-story structure, where Sam Brannan kept a store. . . . There was a rush from the mines, coming after stores, or to have a grand carouse. All had gold dust, and nearly all drank whisky. It was no uncommon occurrence to see a miner call up every person around and spend an ounce or two in treating."[6]

William Lewis Manly was a young man when he left Vermont for the West. He met up with a team of Missouri emigrants and made his way to California. He and another fellow traveler arrived at Coloma and were shocked, like many were, at the way

Saloons were the epicenter of the West, especially in mining towns, as they were a source of information, entertainment, and companionship. Circa 1882. LIBRARY OF CONGRESS

business was conducted. He recalled, "We camped at Coloma all night. Mr. Bradford got his mule shod and paid sixteen dollars, or in the mining phrase, an ounce of gold dust. I visited the small town and found that the only lively business place in it was a large gambling house, and I saw money (gold dust) liberally used—sometimes hundreds of dollars bet on a single card. . . . The game called Monte seemed to be the favorite. . . . Mr. W. M. Stockton, who left his family in Los Angeles, came with Mr. Bennett and went to work with us. As everything here was very high we concluded to let Mr. Stockton take the team and go to Sacramento for provisions for our own use. Flour and meat were each fifty cents a pound, potatoes twenty-five cents a pound and onions one dollar and twenty-five cents each. Onions and potatoes eaten raw were considered very necessary to prevent and cure scurvy, which was quite a common complaint. Whiskey, if not watered, cost one dollar a drink." Manly also remembered the saloon near their claim: "In the creek bottom Mr. Bush of Missouri had a saloon. The building was made mainly of brush, with a split piece for a counter, and another one for a shelf for his whiskey keg, a box of cigars, a few decks of cards and half a dozen glasses, which made up the entire stock of trade for the shop. In front was a table made of two puncheons with a blanket thrown over all, and a few rough seats around. There was no roof except the brush, and through the dry season none was needed except for shade." Manly left Coloma and went to Sacramento, where he found that whiskey and gambling were the only things in abundance, with a glass of whiskey costing fifty cents.[7]

Gold rush pioneer Heinrich Lienhard recalled the level of drinking at Sutter's Mill. He said,

The impudence and boldness of the gold prospectors of that day was unbelievable. They were not afraid to tear down fences to get food for hungry mules and horses, and many harvests were ruined in this manner. I recall one time when I was

*standing near the south gate of the fort, and saw two men
come up on horseback, saddles bulging with the usual equipment carried by miners. They approached at a brisk gallop
and called, "Hello, stranger! What road do we take to the gold
mines?" "Take any road. They all go to the mines," I replied.
Touching spurs to their horses like madmen, they galloped
swiftly away. They whooped and yelled; the pans, bowls, and
picks rattled noisily. Performances of this kind occurred every
day. The poor horses were forced to travel at top speed, as their
riders shouted, bellowed, sang, or cursed. This happened even
more frequently when they were returning from the mines,
if there were gold with which to buy drinks. Strong liquor
was popular, and the miners drank greedily. Whiskey bottles
ceased to be a curiosity, being found everywhere in the streets,
along streams and rivers, and around houses. Enormous piles
of them accumulated inside the fort, which was the rendezvous
for miners and prospectors going out to the mines. This was the
place, too, where men who had mined hundreds or thousands
of dollars' worth of gold congregated when they returned from
the diggings, the place where they attempted to atone for recent
hardships by enormous quantities of alcohol.*[8]

The saloon business in the booming Old West was a good
one—all a man needed was a tent, some glasses, or in some cases
a ladle and a barrel, and whiskey.

Many of the largest silver and gold deposits were found in
the mountainous regions of northern California, Colorado, Montana, Idaho, and Nevada. After the California gold rush began
in 1849, the next big strike was the discovery of the Comstock
Lode in Virginia City, Nevada, which was home to one of the
largest silver strikes in US history. In 1859 silver was discovered
and people raced to get there. The town was founded as part of
Utah Territory and incorporated under Utah, before Nevada came
into existence as a territory in March 1861. By 1862 Virginia City

had a population of close to three thousand miners, madams, and whiskey-drinking souls. Close to its peak in 1875, this bonanza town was home to nearly twenty thousand pioneers. After the organization of the Nevada Territory under the general laws of Utah, the charter of Virginia City was amended to move away from Utah law and conform more closely to the habits and customs of its citizens. Section 8 granted powers to the Trustees, and the words "and providing for licensing bars at which spirituous liquors are sold" were underlined. In 1881 Myron Angel published a book titled *History of the State of Nevada*. In it he wrote, "The authorities of Utah never encourage the sale of liquors, never permit it if possible to prevent it. Of course, this was impossibility from the very commencement with such a population as made up Virginia City. 'Whiskey or death' would have been a rallying cry to rouse the whole population."

This thriving and prosperous silver mining community was home to Mark Twain, aka Samuel Clemens. In 1847 Clemens was apprenticed to a printer, and he also wrote for his brother's newspaper. He later worked as a licensed Mississippi riverboat pilot, but the Civil War put an end to the steamboat traffic and Clemens moved to Virginia City where he edited the *Territorial Enterprise*. On February 3, 1863, "Mark Twain" was born when Clemens signed a humorous travel account with that pseudonym. He arrived in Virginia City in September 1862, and in his book *Roughing It*, he wrote that this booming mining town was the "livest town, for its age and population, that America had ever produced." He also wrote, "The sidewalks swarmed with people—to such an extent, indeed, that it was generally no easy matter to stem the human tide. The streets themselves were just as crowded with quartz wagons, freight teams and other vehicles. The procession was endless. So great was the pack, that buggies frequently had to wait half an hour for an opportunity to cross the principal street. Joy sat on every countenance, and there was a glad, almost fierce, intensity in every eye, that told of the money-getting schemes that were seething in every brain and the high hope that held sway in every heart. Money was as plenty as dust; every individual considered himself wealthy, and a melancholy countenance was nowhere to be seen. There were military companies, fire companies, brass bands, banks, hotels, theatres, 'hurdy-gurdy houses,' wide-open gambling palaces, political pow wows, civic processions, street fights, murders, inquests, riots, a whisky mill every fifteen steps . . . a dozen breweries and half a dozen jails and stationhouses in full operation, and some talk of building a church. The 'flush times' were in magnificent flower!" He later wrote, "The cheapest way to become an influential man and be looked upon by the community at large was to stand behind a bar, wear a cluster diamond pin and sell whiskey. I am not sure but that the saloonkeeper had a shade higher rank than any other member of society. His opinion had weight."

Twain commented that there was a whiskey mill every fifteen steps in his lively silver city. He was not exaggerating; the number of establishments where one could get a drink of whiskey was over seventy in 1864 for the twenty thousand people who lived there. Four of them were owned by women. They offered drinking, gambling, music, and food. One of those saloons, the El Dorado on C Street, advertised, "Shell oysters always on hand. Hot lunch from 11 to 3 p.m., every day."[9, 10]

In 1860 the promise of gold nuggets would once again send prospectors and entrepreneurs to the West Coast. This time it was in Washington Territory to the Oro Fino mines. According to a newspaper story, E. D. Pierce and his partners camped under the stars with a Nez Perce Indian who told them about a gold ball that was embedded in a rock. The Nez Perce believed it was great medicine, but they couldn't extract it from the rock. The next day,

Pierce saw the evidence for himself and, excited about what he had seen, immediately organized a scouting party. They quickly discovered gold in a stream, and by 1861 a rush of pioneers arrived in the area. Some twenty-five or thirty thousand pioneers made their way to the area in May 1862. A town was formed and named Pierce City in honor of its discoverer. As with most mining camps, goods were in short supply and high demand. Flour cost $1 per pound, green tea was $1.25 per pound, blasting powder was $2 per pound, and whiskey sold at $5 to $6 per gallon.[11, 12]

The *Oregonian* in Portland was interested in what was happening in the Upper Columbia region, so it sent a correspondent to report back about what it was like to journey into this new gold mining area. It's likely this writer was Israel Mitchell, who had sent other accounts to the *Oregonian*. He followed the Columbia River to what was described as the Oro Fino Creek, where the mines were located. The newspaper captured the story: "Three miles up the creek is 'Whisky Flat'—a place noted for the astonishing effects of its whiskey. They call this fluid 'Tarantula Juice,' or 'Extract of Scorpions.'" The reporter continued his journey to Oro Fino City, or "Muttonville," as it was called, and after twelve miles reached Quartz Creek. A mile later he came across "Virginia's house of entertainment where she was planting a garden and potatoes." He finally arrived at "Bummer's Hill," which overlooked Oro Fino Flat. Nearby was Pierce City, where about twenty log homes had been built and was about fifteen or twenty feet above Oro Fino Creek. The writer continued, "We are now in the center of the new mines, with ears and mouth open to swallow those 'truly fabulous' reports which are constantly buzzed about the street."[13]

Israel Mitchell reported another account two days later about the Nez Perce mines. He claimed that the "El Dorado" along the Oro Fino and its tributaries, Quartz Creek, Canal Gulch, and Rhodes Fork, included about seven hundred claims, paying from eight to fifty dollars per day. At the time of his visit, Oro Fino

City contained about sixty houses, with more going up every day; there were nine or ten stores, "more saloons than are needed," two blacksmiths, two butcher shops, three families, and about five hundred inhabitants who lived in tents and camps. But by the summer of 1864 Oro Fino was declining. A report stated it was rather gloomy and only a few hardy souls remained. Three stores and several saloons and whiskey shops were all that was left.[14, 15]

Grasshopper Creek in what is now Montana was the site of another big find in the summer of 1862. By 1863 three thousand people lived in camps and settlements established in the area, including the town of Bannack. In May 1865 a fire devastated the town. After the fire the *Sacramento Union* published this report: "It presents a most ludicrous appearance right now. Impromptu whisky stands, restaurants tables all in the open air, tents, blankets on crop poles, etc. although not a 'new thing' to the Californian, is a cause of 'wonderment' to the webfoot." Sam Jaggers was a wholesale liquor distributor in Bannack during the 1860s and was interviewed by the *Dillon Examiner* in Montana about his life there. Sam recalled his days in Bannack fondly, from rotgut whiskey to high wines, which was distilled alcohol; and more, he told a story of life in a mining community and how whiskey was a great influencer:

> *In the summer of '66 I was in Bannack and having some few stray dollars at my command I made a deal with James Harvey for the retail liquor establishment he conducted, which was at that time one of the best places in the camp. It had a first-class bar, not one of the hand-made ones like the majority of the saloons of pioneer days had, but it had real oak furniture and a real plate glass mirror behind the bar. Bannack was still a town of considerable importance in those days, in spite of the fact that the capital had been moved to Virginia City [Montana] and that the placer mines of old Alder gulch were eclipsing anything ever discovered in the world. Traffic in the*

hard liquor line was pretty good during all of the time I was in the business. All kinds of drinks sold for two bits each and it was very seldom that we ever had to take anything except gold dust for our stuff and no saloon or other business place at that time was complete unless it was equipped with gold scales. Whiskey sold at the rate of $4 a quart, when bought in that quantity, and wines brought $10 a bottle. I now want to tell you boys something about the way we made our liquors in the early days and I am sure that you will not give it away. All of our liquors at that time came from Los Angeles, California, and they were freighted in wagons all the way from where they were made in the Golden State to the various mining camps of Montana. When they left California, mind you, they were not in the shape of whiskey or rum, but were high wines and I guess all of you have heard something about that fiery liquor. Once the high wines had been safely landed in our cellars, us saloon keepers of the early days set about making the various liquors demanded by the horny-handed miners who were delving in the placer mines all over the territory. If a man wanted any kind of liquor he got it, and it did not make any difference whether he asked for whiskey, brandy, rum, gin or some brand of wine, he got it and all came originally from the same barrel. With the aid of fusil oil, which cost us $5 an ounce in St. Louis, we could make any kind of liquor a man wanted out of the high wines and to tell you the truth, although it might be my imagination, I believe we had a whole lot better whiskey in the early days than we have at present. In 1867 there was a whiskey famine in the territory and for a while it seemed as if a dire calamity was staring the country in the face. Bannack was in line with the rest of Montana and the indications were that the town would have to be a dry one through the force of circumstances. Finally I heard of two barrels of whiskey that were on the market in the town of Deer Lodge and I lost no time in getting over *there after them. I made the journey on horseback and I made my pony fairly burn up the ground between Bannack and the Cottonwood. Arriving there I speedily made a deal for the two barrels of whiskey, paying $750 in clean gold dust for them. One of the barrels was good stuff and the other one was positively the worst liquor I ever sampled. It was rot-gut of the rankest kind, but the boys at Bannack wanted whiskey of some kind and I was bound they should have it. However, I thought that I could evolve a scheme to make drinkable whiskey out of the rot-gut, so I extended my journey to Virginia City and purchased from John Rockwell two cases of peaches and had them shipped on the coach to Bannack. When I got home found that the whiskey had arrived ahead of me and I began making my arrangements to convert the rot-gut into good liquor. The peaches I dumped into a tub and with the aid of a big mallet I converted them into a pulp. This pulp I poured into the rot-gut barrel and then had my three clerks take turns in rolling the barrel up and down the cellar. For 24 hours they kept this up without stopping for a minute and the result was that it was converted into a whiskey that the miners would walk ten miles, after the close of a hard day's work, in order to pay 25 cents for a sample of it. At that time we got our beer from George D. French, father of our efficient clerk of the court, and the old gentleman charged us $16 for a four gallon-keg. I got back at him once, however, while I had this keg of converted rot-gut. He had heard of the good barrel of whiskey that Jaggers had secured at Deer Lodge and one night he brought his jug down to have it filled. I looked wise and charged him $16 for the gallon. He just went up in the air at the price and I told him that it was a poor day when a gallon of whiskey was not worth a gallon of beer. "Sugar and pie!" said the old man, "that is outrageous, but I have just got to have that whiskey," and he took it. Before spring all of the whiskey was gone and the business of the saloon was confined to the beer made by Mr. French* and champagne which had come from California. When the whiskey gave out I had 50 baskets of champagne in the cellar. It had cost me $50 a case in Los Angeles, four quarts, and I sold it for $10 a bottle in Bannack. Occasionally Bannack saw a touch of old time excitement in her latter days while I was conducting the saloon. At one time a large influx of women came to the town and they did not make enough money to keep them in meal tickets. They just had to do something or starve and one evening a committee of three, one of them, being a fine looker, called on me and asked for permission to conduct a hurdy-gurdy in my saloon. I told the women that I would take the matter under advisement for a day, until I had consulted the business men of the town, and then give them an answer. The next day I talked with the principal business men of the town about the plan and they were all more than anxious to have a dance ball added to Bannack's attractions. Accordingly, I told the girls the next day that they could have the bar-room three nights out of the week for a dance hall and the following night, with "Banjo Bill" to furnish the music, the hurdy-gurdy was opened. It was a success from the start and the bar did a thriving business, too. Each dance cost a dollar and of that amount the bar gets four bits worth of drinks and the girl got a ticket calling for 50 cents. On one occasion the good-looking girl, who was on the committee which broached the subject to me, cashed in $50 worth of tickets when settling time came after an unusually lively night. During the time I was in business Yank Williams, who died a few years ago in Bannack, was taking out hundreds of dollars daily, in the phenomenal find he had made in the canyon below Marys-ville. Yank had big ideas at that time and the wealth of gold which was pouring into his gold dust sacks evidently turned his head, for he had one man employed whose sole duty was to go to Bannack every day and buy a gallon of whiskey for Mr. Williams and his miners. He was paid $6 a day for this

duty, too. Another man, he hailed from Boston I think, had a
quart bottle sent down to his cabin in Marysville every day
and, every once in a while, I would send him his bill and he
would give me his check on the Virginia City bank, which was
then our nearest financial institution. But the good old days
of Bannack passed away; the saloon I conducted was destroyed
by fire and I moved away."[16]

Despite Jaggers's comment about there being a whiskey shortage in Virginia City, one man managed to acquire enough whiskey to find himself before the judge to explain himself. It was election day in February 1867, and this "unfortunate" celebrated a bit too much. When the judge asked him why he drank too much, he claimed the water was poisonous and he had no choice. His statement read, "It is a known fact to all well-informed people, that the water of this region is heavily charged with poisonous matter, in passing through the earth, containing, as it does, large quantities of antimony, arsenic, etc. The injurious effects of these poisons upon the system is too well known to demand any illustration or argument at the present time." He went on to argue that when the water was used to boil potatoes, coffee, meat, and other edibles, the poisons were mostly removed. He stated that drinking the water straight was foolish and damn near suicidal. "For this reason I avoid it on all occasions when it is compatible with my feelings and the condition of my exchequer. The whisky of this place is, on election days, especially when it comes in connection with Chinese new year, highly preferable in a hygienic and financial point of view; therefore I imbibed somewhat too freely of the stimulating fluid, and in endeavoring to enlighten one of my benighted opponents by giving him freely a lecture on heads, in the presence of a large and highly intelligent audience, I was shamefully interrupted by a member of the 'Star' club and ruthlessly dragged into the presence of your honor." Fortunately for him, the judge dismissed him without costs.[17]

Hamilton, Nevada, held the next mining discovery in Nevada and boomed in 1868. It was located over the low Pancake Mountain, across a narrow valley, and a long winding canyon, which led up into the White Pine Mountain Range. The March 1869 issue of *Overland Monthly* described the place: "Long lines of mules and oxen, drawing heavy wagons, laden with supplies of every kind: mill machinery, whiskey, provisions, whiskey, hardware, whiskey, mule feed, and whiskey again—jerkwater' stages, which had been three or four days making the trip of one hundred and ten miles from Hamilton with passengers for the mines; mine owners, or those who had but recently sold mines, and were flush, on horseback; bull-whackers, in soldiers' coats, with whips a dozen feet in length on poles longer still, just in from Austin or Wadsworth; honest miners, with salted claims, ready to sell to the newly-arrived greenhorns; foot packers, without a cent, who had packed their blankets and luggage all the way from Elko, sparing their meals, and sleeping in snow drifts, if they slept at all; painted Jezebels from every mining camp from Idaho to Sonora; Shoshone Indians, Chinamen, and 'capitalists,' who in San Francisco were never known as men with plethoric bank accounts, crowded the streets of Hamilton."

Whiskey played a crucial role in mining communities, and the *Overland Monthly* made note of it in their story on Hamilton.

All was bustle and hurry, noise, excitement, and confusion. The stores and saloons were crowded with men in huge overcoats, the pockets of which were filled with big specimens, small silver bars, and rolls of location notices and assay certificates, buying, selling, and talking mines, and "bummers" of the seediest class, who drank at the expense of every stranger who approached the bar—swore, talked, fought, and "swapped" filthy lies from morning to night. In the evening the streets were deserted, but the mad excitement indoors was as great as ever. The bartenders were kept in incessant motion in their frantic efforts to supply the demand for drinks which poured in from every direction. . . . The dance-house was filled with half or wholly tipsy miners, with a sprinkling of abandoned women, whose smiles and favors were as eagerly sought for and as jealously observed by the unfavored as were ever those of the most gifted and virtuous of their sex in the abode of wealth and refinement, at the East, on a gala night.

In the rear of every barroom was a door bearing a sign inscribed "Club Room," through which was heard the strains of discordant music and the chinking of coin. These club rooms were crowded to their utmost capacity, and the tables were piled with coin and checks, while hundreds of men, who had made lucky strikes at finding, working, or, more frequently, selling mines, were betting away in a single hour what might have kept them, and those dependent on them, for years in comfort, or served as the foundation for a colossal fortune. Every five or ten minutes the dealers would pause in their work of turning cards and raking down the coin to ring a bell, when a bartender would enter the club room. "Gentlemen, what will you take? You drink with me, you know!" said the smiling dealer in pasteboard and other people's hard-earned coin. "Whiskey toddy! Whiskey straight! Whiskey hot! Whiskey sour! Whiskey and gum!" replied the crowd; the fiery liquor was swallowed, and the game went on.[18]

Nearby Treasure City, California, was also a mining town whose residents were "forced" to drink whiskey because the water was so bad. The *Steamer Alta California* made note of it in their mining town reports: "On Treasure Hill there is not a drop of water except what is made of snow melted over fires and is peddled around at 25 cents for small buckets. . . . This snow water produces irrigation of the bowels and is considered dangerous if used too freely. Whiskey is recommended in its place. In justice to the people of the district we must say that they generally show a disposition to manually conquer their prejudices, and restating the temptation to indulge in water swallow whiskey instead with as much grace as if they liked it from the start."[19] The snowy, mountainous town of Park City, Utah, was also being mined for silver. It could be argued that Brigham Young and his followers were partly responsible for founding Park City. In 1862 federal troops were sent to protect Young, and while there, Colonel Patrick Connor sent his troops out to search for valuable minerals to entice others to the area to "thin out" the Mormon population. Six years later, when troops were climbing over the Big Cottonwood Canyon, they discovered silver and named their first mine the Flagstaff. By 1870 the town was named Parley's Park, for the man who had a toll road there years before, and had a population of 164. By 1872 the town was renamed Park City, and the Ontario Mine, which produced over fifty million dollars during its existence, was located.[20]

Most of the towns that sprang up out west were spurred by explorations, trading, mining, cattle, railroads, and pioneers. Saloons were often the first to appear and the last to go. This image shows one of the great fires that came through the mining town of Park City, Utah, in 1898. The first business to rise from the ashes was George Wanning's saloon. PARK CITY MUSEUM

While mining reigned in the Rocky Mountains and the Pacific Northwest, cattle was king on the plains. Cattle drives from southern Texas up to Kansas were thriving. There were numerous cattle trails all over the West, with a large portion of them originating in Texas. One of the most frequently used trails in the late 1860s was the Chisholm Trail, which ran from the vast cattle grazing lands in southern Texas, through Oklahoma, and into Kansas. Other trails could be found in New Mexico, Montana Territory, Dakota Territory, Wyoming, Nebraska, and Missouri.

The trails were long and dusty, and cowboys were in their saddles for three to four months during the drives. Cowboys did indeed drink, but most did not dare drink while on the job, whether it be working on the ranch rounding up cattle or out on the trails. Trail bosses and chuckwagon cooks would send a

Cowboys sometimes crossed the line and became outlaws, such as the famous Butch Cassidy and his Wild Bunch gang, who were notorious for stealing horses and robbing trains as well as saloons. The saloon was also one of their hangouts. Standing is Harry Longabaugh (the Sundance Kid); the man sitting on the chair beside him is Butch Cassidy. Circa 1889, Utah. UTAH STATE HISTORICAL SOCIETY

drunken cowboy packing faster than a bronco bucks its rider. Cowboys, often called "waddies," needed to be sober and able to walk a straight line because their jobs were dangerous and required long hours. Too many lives—both human and animal—depended upon a sober head. The only person on roundups or on the trail with whiskey was the chuckwagon cook. Oftentimes the cook might stash a secret bottle of whiskey for his personal use in case of "snakebites."

There was a strong belief—or maybe just a good excuse—that whiskey was a true cure for snakebites. Whether on the cattle trail or out hunting or fishing, whiskey went along for the journey. Pioneers thought an ounce of prevention was worth a pound of cure in the "serpent-infested" country. An 1880s newspaper story noted that "preliminary doses of 'medicine' has always been essential to the sportsman in case of calamity. How many total abstainers have we seen hunting in vain for a snake to bite them. The whiskey cure is the most popular remedy now before the public, but, alas! It is a quack nostrum; it does not cure snake bites, it does not even help to cure them in some cases." The writers argued that whiskey did not help, but actually may have been responsible for a man's death. In fact, the man was intoxicated when he got bit by the snake and was then dosed again. The doctors said the whiskey killed him, and the paper concluded, "Liquor is undoubtedly a valuable agent in serpent bites, but sufficient only should be given to arrest the action of the virus; more than that causes alcoholic poisoning, which is as fatal as the fangs of a serpent."[21]

Cowboys didn't have to worry about being overdosed with the snakebite cure because they had to wait until the end of the trail to get drunk—in fact, parching their dusty throats was something that kept them focused on reaching the end. From the 1860s to the 1880s, Abilene, Caldwell, Dodge City, Newton, Trail City, and Wichita, Kansas, as well as towns in Texas, saw many a cowboy and thousands of cattle roar into town in late summer.

The cowboy era lasted just two decades (1860s–1880s), but nostalgi-cally represents the romance of the wide-open range before barbed wire. Railroad or end-of-trail towns along the Chisholm Trail included Dodge City, Abilene, and Ellsworth in Kansas. Pueblo and Denver, Colorado, and Chey-enne, Wyoming, were at the end of the Goodnight Loving Trail. The Cattle Exchange saloon's name captures the era. Cisco, Texas, 1880s. CENTRAL UNIVERSITY LIBRARIES, SOUTHERN METHODIST UNIVERSITY

When the cowboys reached these cow towns, a mighty cele-bration took place. They wanted women, meals that didn't consist of beans, clean clothes, hot baths, and a goodly amount of whiskey at one of the saloons in town. Being on a dusty trail for months with only men and cows for companions, combined with a newly acquired wad of money, led to loud and wild celebrations. Because of their rowdy, celebratory behavior and a few bad hombres, the townspeople didn't like the cowboys and they gained a bad reputation. When the trail-weary cowboys got a bit too wild in town, they would drunkenly holler at the moon, shoot at the shimmering glasses stacked behind the bar, or even shoot out the town's gas lights. However, the next day, the sober shooters returned to the scene of their crime, apologized to the owner, and asked to pay for the damages. With actions like those, it's understandable why so many cow towns had bad reputations. But despite what you see in the movies, most cowboys had honor.

Still, there were stories of wild and raucous behavior from many of the cow towns. Former Texas resident Mrs. Emma Falconer recalled, "A special stunt of the cowboys was to ride into the saloon and shoot a barrel of whiskey until they could take a glass and catch their drink, then ride away and the next day return and tell the owner to put his price on the damage. This has happened here in Marlin and some of the oldest families' boys have been among the number, but who, as they grew to manhood made law-abiding citizens."[22]

Despite what the cowboys did in a town, everyone knew their presence meant revenue. By 1871 officials in Ellsworth, Kansas, along with the Kansas Pacific Railway, had put up cattle pens and let the Texas cattle ranchers know they were ready for their cattle and cowboys. The town's permanent residents numbered from seven to eight hundred, but the population would swell during the cattle drives. Two years later Ellsworth hit its stride, and the town saw some 220,000 head of cattle. Of course, once the cattle were loaded, the cowboys were free to spend their hard-earned cash. It was estimated they earned about fifty dollars per drive. Keep in mind that drinks cost one or two bits (12½ cents and 25 cents, respectively). Cattle buyers from Colorado, Nebraska, the Dakotas, Missouri, and Iowa filled up the local hotels and saloons during cattle buying season. Kansas's *Daily Commonwealth* wrote a detailed description of Ellsworth in 1873: "Having seen all the sights of the theatre we will direct our steps toward the 'Drover's Cottage,' and seek repose, leaving the inevitable dance house for less susceptible parties to visit. On our way home we pass by scores of gambling hells and whisky shops, all in full blast. Strange as it may seem, but little drunkenness and disorder is apparent. This is owing to the perfect police regulations." Despite its hopeful prospects and good police force, Ellsworth was out of the cattle business by 1875, and the cows were being driven to and loaded on cattle cars in Dodge City, Kansas.[23]

Dodge City, Kansas, was laid out in July 1872, under the supervision of A. A. Robinson, who was the chief engineer of

Ellsworth, Kansas, was the end of the trail for cowboys on the long cattle drives. Circa 1867. LIBRARY OF CONGRESS

the Atchison, Topeka & Santa Fe Railway. The town company, which was set up to develop Dodge, consisted of Colonel Richard I. Dodge, commander of the post at Fort Dodge, and several of the officers who were under him. Dodge City was located five miles west of Fort Dodge, on the north bank of the Arkansas River. The Atchison, Topeka & Santa Fe railroad reached Dodge City in the early part of September the same year. Dodge City became a supply center for buffalo hunters, cowboys, and traders, and was where the cattle trails ended. It was in this town that Bat Masterson and Wyatt Earp gained reputations as good lawmen. Men with their character and daring were highly sought after and needed in a town where cowboys dusted off their shirts and quenched their thirsts.

The Honorable Robert M. Wright lived in Dodge City during its boom days and later wrote a book about life in his "wicked" town. He claimed his town was not the worst place in the West and said Virginia City, Nevada, was way worse. He included a newspaper article from the *Topeka Times* that described Dodge City in 1873. He wrote, "During the year of 1873 we roughed it in the West. Our first stopping place was the famous Dodge City, at the time a perfect paradise for gamblers, cut-throats, and girls. On our first visit the buildings in the town were not buildings, with one or two exceptions, but tents and dugouts. Everyone in town, nearly, sold whisky or kept a restaurant, perhaps both. The Atchison, Topeka & Santa Fe Railway was just then working its way up the low banked Arkansas, and Dodge was the frontier town."[24]

Either Wright was exaggerating or things had dramatically changed by 1878 when Dodge City had about six hundred people living in it with about fifteen businesses that sold liquor. In 1880 the population doubled, but the places to buy booze shrank to about ten.[25, 26] Another man named George Romspert recalled Dodge City as "the most wicked place." In his book, *The Western Echo*, which was published in 1881, he recalled how the cowboys acted when they got to town:

There are saloons all along the railroads and cattle-trails, and when the boys are out alone upon the range for some time they feel like having a picnic when getting to where somebody lives. They are usually very liberal when they have money, and everybody present is called on to "come up and represent." Whisky is considered the grace of God in this country, and of course it is very seldom refused. Now, if there are several together, a few drinks about makes happiness full; and the ball then opens. The boys all draw good wages, their expenses are light, and most of them aim to spend in saloons every dollar that is not needed for actual necessaries. They often draw from fifty to one hundred dollars at once, and spend every dollar of it before leaving a saloon. There are men making fortunes off the cow-boys today. There are professional gamblers lurking around most of these frontier saloons, and they watch to intoxicate the boys and then play them out of their money. Though the game be begun in the best of humor, it is usual for each man to lay his six-shooter at his side; and the maxim is, mind your eye. As long as everything is done squarely there is no trouble; but the first man that is caught tricking is in hot quarters; and I have seen some deadly battles without one word spoken. Sometimes the gamblers entirely strip the boys, and with an understanding, when there is a large pot, they point the six-shooters at the gamblers' heads and pull in the pile. Some years ago Dodge City, Kansas, was given up to be the roughest and most wicked place in the United States. It is situated right where the Texas trail crosses the railroad, and was a regular stock-center. Numbers of cow-boys were constantly going in and out, and whole dens of gamblers and prostitutes were quartered here for lucre. The population being composed of such beings, and the clash of the six-shooter being the voice of the law, the vilest consequences are but natural. Ah! many a man played his last game here, and mingled his dying-breath with the lurid smoke of the six-shooters. Men *were shot down like dogs, and buried as they fell, red with gore and horribly mangled. There is at this place a yard called the Boot Grave-yard, a place well known to all western men, and called thus from the fact that thirty-eight men have been buried here with their boots on. There was scarcely a day that there was not a riot in town among the cow-boys, or between the cow-boys and gamblers; and of course shooting and cutting was the consequence. Emigrants passing through with wagons, and not knowing the place, were decoyed into dark places and robbed. Passengers from the trains, on going in for refreshments and showing any amount of money, were trapped and robbed, and were killed upon resistance. You are a stranger in the country, and they are all cliqued together; and what are you to do? If you go to making much trouble, or get to shooting off your mouth, the consequences can be imagined. Even when there are officers, they are not able to command order; for the first day they try it a ball from some unknown villain will strike him. Hence the officers are usually cliqued with the desperadoes. The easier a person can get out of these places the better; for the officers themselves will put you into a dungeon for the gamblers to rob you.*[27]

Because of incidents associated with whiskey and drunkenness, a Kansas constitutional amendment that prohibited "the manufacture and sale of intoxicating liquors" was ratified by a majority of the voters in November 1880, and took effect on January 1, 1881. The Kansas Legislature also passed a law that made manufacturing alcohol a misdemeanor, which took effect May 1, 1881. A Kansas newspaper was not happy with the new prohibition bill so they placed this notice: "We have the statement upon reliable authority, that the twelve saloon keepers of Dodge City have made up a purse of $1200 and deposited it in a bank, with the endorsement on the certificate that it is to be paid, 'to the widow of the s-n of a b—h who informs on the saloon men.' Here is an opportunity for some enterprising woman who possesses a husband of the kind described, and who wishes to get rid of him."[28]

The ratio of places to buy liquor in Dodge City remained steady, and in 1883 there were roughly fifteen saloons, hotels, and restaurants where whiskey could be procured by its 1,500 residents.[29] Most of the citizens of Dodge City, Kansas, didn't pay any attention to the prohibition laws until 1885 when cities across Kansas reaffirmed their commitment to enforcing the laws. Dodge City resident and judge Robert Wright fought the bill and later concluded, "In the spring of 1885, preparations were made for the enforcement of the Prohibitory Liquor Law in Dodge City, and the sale of eighty barrels of four-year-old whisky, besides other liquors and bar fixtures was announced by Henry Sturm, the well-known purveyor of the city. The prohibition law put a different character on liquor sales, many of the saloons being transformed into 'drug stores.'"

Once the Texas and Pacific Railway reached Fort Worth, Texas, in 1876, Texas cattle drivers who used to go through Kansas along the Chisholm Trail no longer needed to move their cattle to places like Dodge City. Instead they went up the trail to Fort Worth and shipped them from there. Fort Worth soon became the new bustling cow town where cowboys spent their pay quenching their parched throats with whiskey. Tom J. Snow was a bartender in Fort Worth during the 1880s, and he remembered many tense encounters. "At the time I worked as a bartender, Fort Worth was a pure cow town. Cowboys and ranchers, by the score, visited Fort Worth, bent on business and pleasure. My experience back of the bar, while waiting on the cowboys and ranchers, was interesting and enjoyable. For one to be successful as a dealer with the cowhands, it was necessary to take the fellows as they presented themselves. However, one could always depend on the cowmen playing fair." Snow continued, "It wasn't just the high-born who enjoyed elaborate mixed drinks, however." He recalled how cowboys would ask for his priciest fare, at any hour of the day: "One morning five waddies walked into the saloon and called for a 'frosty cocktail.' This particular drink was in great favor at the time and was among the expensive drinks. I mixed the five drinks and set the cocktails on the bar. The boys drank with great relish, and commended me on my ability as a mixer of the cocktail."[30]

Norway native Andre Jorgenson Anderson was another Fort Worth pioneer who settled there in 1874. He recalled the range of establishments that greeted visitors in the up-and-coming town of Fort Worth.

The White Elephant was the most magnificent place in Fort Worth those days. It was located between Third and Fourth Streets on Main. It was a saloon, gambling house, and restaurant. There were no queens connected with the White Elephant. Before its opening, the place was advertised to be one of the finest combination saloons, gambling houses and restaurants, without any exceptions. Those days ladies did not frequent saloons, but the good ladies of Fort Worth could not resist taking a look at the White Elephant during its opening night, and a large number came to look at the place. Upon entering the White Elephant, the people saw a filigree mahogany wood bar and back bar. All the glassware was cut glass of the highest grade, and stacked high on the back bar. There was a large display of imported and domestic wines, liquors and cordials. The bartenders were dressed immaculately and in white jackets, shirts, collars and bow ties. Leading from the bar room was a wide stairway running to the second floor where the gambling room was located. On this stairway was laid the very best of carpet. At the entrance to the gambling room was a medium size table on which was stacked gold and silver coins, standing about six inches high. A uniformed man stood guard at this table. The men selected to run the various gambling games were chosen for their good looks as well as

*ability to operate a game. The excellent appearance of these
men was the general talk among the ladies. Every game oper-
ator was dressed in a suit custom-made from the highest grade
of cloth. They wore white stiff-front shirts with a conspicuous
diamond stud in the bosom, a conspicuous diamond ring on
their finger, and the charm, which hung from their watch
chain, also contained a diamond. Those men were groomed in
the latest of the day. . . . There was no charge for drinks to the
patrons of the gambling room, and there were no restrictions
to the kind of drinks served. The rule was to let the patrons
drink and be merry, because the devices controlling the gaming tables took care of the proprietors. In addition, the more
the patrons drank the more reckless they became with their
money. Therefore, the free drinks were a good investment.*[31]

Anderson then shifted his thoughts down the sliding scale
of opulence to another establishment in the third ward, better
known as Hell's Half Acre. Not far from the stockyards was a
small section near the railroad dubbed Hell's Half Acre because
of its bad reputation. Hell's Half Acre was a term that was used
in many towns across the West to describe the section of town
that deplorable and unsavory characters called home. The saloons
plied their patrons with cheap whiskey and dens of iniquity. Fort
Worth's Hell's Half Acre was the most well-known and could be
found within the borders of 9th or 10th Streets down to the Texas
and Pacific railroad. Front Street (now Lancaster Avenue) was the
south boundary, on the west, Throckmorton, and on the east, Rusk
(now Commerce).

Anderson recalled that area all too well. "At the other end of
the saloon grade was the First and Last Chance saloon. It was
located on Front Street across from the old depot. This was the
place the 'cinches' patronized. It was the kind of a place patronized
by the fellow who felt at home where he could expectorate [spit]
on the floor at will, where he could sit down on the floor or lie

Hells Half Acre, 1893, in Oklahoma Territory. Note the Red Light Saloon in the background. This camp later became the more permanent town of Perry, Oklahoma. NATIONAL ARCHIVES

down in a corner, and if one became too drunk for locomotion there was a room where one was placed until sobered. This saloon had one large room used for placing the drunks. The room contained no furniture and men just lay on the floor. I have seen this drunker's room packed like sardines in a can."[32]

Hell's Half Acre had plenty of saloons that offered bad whiskey, which George Watkins of Missouri found out the hard way. He mistakenly strayed into the confines of the "Acre" and visited a saloon where he ordered whiskey. He was given a concoction that was not whiskey and later robbed of the $175 in his pocketbook, which was a common practice by a certain element in the Acre. When questioned, he stated he could not remember where or with whom he had been drinking.[33]

Thrill-seeking William Bentley from East Texas had heard all about the Acre and wanted to see it firsthand. When he arrived in Fort Worth, he proceeded to the Acre where he was quickly persuaded to drink and became intoxicated. He was robbed of eighty-five dollars and later told the *Dallas Morning News* that "he had no desire to prosecute any one, saying that any man who was fool enough to go into 'Hell's Half Acre' and drink the stuff sold there, ought to be robbed and then kicked out of town." Sadly, men like Watkins and Bentley weren't the only casualties of the Acre. There were many others who were robbed and beaten. Even Fort Worth's *Gazette* reported, "Greenhorns continue to get robbed in 'Hell's Half Acre.'" [34, 35]

By the 1890s Fort Worth city officials had had enough and were trying to clean up the Acre. A grand jury returned about thirty indictments against property owners who were renting their premises for "immoral" purposes. The keepers of the leading houses of ill-fame and gamblers were also indicted. The "boss" of the third ward was A. G. Rintleman. He was a wealthy saloon owner said to be worth one hundred thousand dollars in 1890. Money didn't matter to the officials in town, and he was convicted that year for robbing a man the previous winter. [36, 37]

Saloons all over the West offered entertainment for cowboys across the frontier. Colorado City, Texas, was a cattle-shipping center, and ranchers drove their cattle to this railroad town from as far north as Amarillo, from as far south as San Angelo, and from eastern New Mexico. Once the cattle were loaded on the train cars, the cowboys enjoyed saloons like Bud Brown's, which was one of about twenty-five in town. Bud remembered, "It was a typical frontier cow town and the town's sole support came from cattlemen. There was an abundance of money. It was not unusual to see a man reach in his pocket and pull out a pouch containing several hundred dollars in $20.00 gold coins." He also recalled a convention in the mid-1880s that netted him large whiskey profits. "The meeting was attended by all the leading ranchers of the district, and many came from distant places. To say that the town was busy waiting on the trade, is stating the situation mildly. There existed a scramble on the part of the visitors to get waited on. My bar was crowded from the hour of opening, till we closed in the wee hours of the morning. Rancher after rancher would come in and call every person in the bar up to 'name their pizen.' When a

This thirsty cowpuncher takes his drink in the doorway of a Colorado saloon circa 1907. LIBRARY OF CONGRESS

rancher gave such order, each bartender would report to me the total charge for the drinks he served. I then would total the bill for the treater, who would place the money, usually in gold coins on the bar. The amounts were from $5.00 to $15.00, and many times more, especially if champagne had been served. Such treats as I have described were not just an occasional happening, but frequent during the convention."[38]

Colorado City declined in the late 1880s when Amarillo was connected to the Fort Worth and Denver Railway and saloons and gambling joints sprang up there. Texas cowboy Richard Murphy recalled the "pizen" in Amarillo: "Some of the boys played the gambling joints, some just soaked themselves in the 'pizen,' and some went sally-hooting in the sally joints. Any kind of a joint that a fellow wanted was in the town to satisfy the waddies' wants. Nearly all the saloons in Amarillo, at that time, had bull-pens at the rear of the joints. The purpose for which the bull-pens were built was to have a place to shunt the fellows who became overloaded where they could sleep off the load of 'pizen;' also, to prevent interference from the law, or meddling gentry who were looking for a chance to swipe a roll of money. The bull-pen was also used for a battle ground. When a couple of fellows got riled at each other, they were shunted into the bull-pen to cool off. The saloon bouncers would take the guns away from the riled men and push them into the bull-pen to settle the argument, bear-fight fashion. That method saved a lot of shooting, but could not be worked in all cases and there was an occasional shooting. When I think of the Amarillo of those days, I recall a big sign that one saloon had in front of its place of business. It read, 'Whiskey, the road to ruin. Come in.'"[39]

Whiskey also played a role in the cowboy's life when he wasn't working. Loneliness, downtime, and celebrations were all occasions to take a swig from a jug. Church socials or country dances were events where a cowboy found some entertainment. Ranch hands often attended these events with the hope of finding a female to dance with or have a conversation. Cowboy Charles Weibush recalled the country dances during the 1880s in McLennan County, Texas: "And there was the country dances! They have disappeared like the ranches that is, the cow-boy dances. It was not an uncommon sight to see the cowboys dancing with a pistol in one pocket and a bottle of whiskey in the other. A fight, before the dance was over, was so common that no one paid any attention to them unless there happened to be blood spilled."

Park City, Utah, had its share of saloons and colorful characters. The *Park Record* made this statement in 1882: "If a fellow wants to become intoxicated he can start in at one end of the street, take a drink at each saloon and store that handles liquors and before he is half way up or down unless he has the capacity of vinegar barrel, be gloriously intoxicated." That might explain why a once beautiful and virtuous woman of Park City fell from grace. Fanny Fulleride was known for frequenting the Park City saloons as often as her male counterparts did. On a warm July day when some Indians were in town, Fanny managed to jump on one of their bareback ponies. One of the Indians managed to get her hat and began waving it around and exclaiming, "I got he hat—he got me horse. Yes, you be, heap fun." Fanny could barely stay on the horse in her drunken state, and when she was finally taken off the horse, she was promptly arrested and put in jail. While she was serving time for her addiction to whiskey in the Coalville jail, Fanny saw a band of vigilantes charging the building. Thinking they were for her, she promised to never drink again. The *Park Record* reported the story: ". . . at present occupying one of the apartments on the charge of drunkenness and disorderly conduct, thought they were after her, and screamed to them to leave her alone, 'For God's sake I'll never drink another drop as long as I live.' If we should see Fanny drunk again we may conclude there is no truth in the report, or she has forgotten her promise."[40, 41, 42]

Park City's mineral discovery and its town's character were no match for those in Deadwood. The Black Hills of the Dakota Territory were home to the Lakota Indians until a rich gold deposit was discovered in the fall of 1875. A tent town quickly emerged and a stampede to Deadwood Gulch took place. Deadwood was a remote, wild and ungoverned town, and the pioneers who resided there did so illegally. The US government had given this land to the Lakotas in 1868 in the Fort Laramie Treaty. That didn't stop excited fortune seekers from illegally entering Indian land, and the population in the fall and winter of 1876 swelled to about ten thousand. Seth Bullock, who became sheriff of Deadwood, arrived in August 1876 and wrote to a friend about the prospects. "I arrived here August 3d and found a 'red hot' mining town. . . . Claims are 300 feet up and down. . . . A great many here are idle and broke. . . . Business of all kinds is represented. [Jack] Lan-grishe has a theatre here, and two dance houses boom nightly. We have no law and order, and no prospect of either. . . . I cannot advise you to come; on the contrary, I think you are doing better than you could here. Board here is $10 per week, flour $8 per hundred, bacon 20 cents per pound, etc., whisky 25 cents a drink."[43]

Early Deadwood resident Jerry Lewis, who was one of James Butler "Wild Bill" Hickok's pallbearers, also recalled the lively gold town in early 1876. He told a reporter: "Four hundred buildings have been erected, and every lot on the town site has the foundation of some sort of structure laid on it. There are four regular saloons, where a bad quality of whisky is retailed, and six stores, where you can buy groceries, clothing, canned fruits, gum boots or whisky. A dance house is to be established soon, in Swarengen Hall, a log and frame building 35 × 80 feet, and a bevy of eight waiter and dance girls are now en route from Cheyenne, their arrival being eagerly and impatiently awaited." E. C. Lott arrived in May and noted the number of places to get a drink of the golden elixir: "Stores are plenty, and so are whisky mills and gambling houses, and hurdy houses are starting." Imperial and Kentucky whiskies were popular when they were available, and Fred Heime offered his patrons Vienna sausages, cheese, herring, and summer bologna at his Union Park saloon. Joseph Pascal & Co. was able to bring in various kinds of whiskey by 1877, which helped replace some of the rotgut that had been served earlier. It was still being sold, but those who struck it lucky in Deadwood could choose from Moon & Bowman's Cold Water, Mercer Co., Edmund H. Taylor Jr's. O.F.C., and Stonewall. Because "real" whiskey was sometimes hard to come by in Deadwood, it was a big deal when barrels rolled into town. Deadwood was difficult to reach by coach, so freight shipments of large barrels was erratic. The *Black Hills Daily Times* wrote in 1882: "An Immense Stock. For a couple of weeks past teams have been unloading an immense stock of wine, beer, and liquors for Gottstein & Franklin. Their stock includes the very best brands of cigars, cordials, pure gin, fine rum, extra brandy and splendid whiskies and last though not least one hundred barrels of genuine Bourbon whisky on hand.... Prices to suit the times."[44, 45, 46]

Deadwood had many colorful characters during its boom, but none are more famous than Martha Jane "Calamity Jane" Cannary and the man she adored, James Butler "Wild Bill" Hickok. Jane was more comfortable around men rather than her female counterparts and had gained a reputation in Deadwood for cussing, spitting tobacco, and getting drunk and disorderly.

Deadwood, South Dakota, was a famous western frontier town known for its celebrated outlaws and lawmen. Wild Bill Hickok, Calamity Jane, and Seth Bullock were just a few who called this raucous town home. Circa 1876. LIBRARY OF CONGRESS

"Wild Bill" Hickok was Deadwood's most famous resident, and he lived there for a time until his sudden death. He was murdered at the No. 10 saloon in 1876 by John "Jack" McCall. After his death Colonel F. G. Patrick recalled Wild Bill while he was in Deadwood and his fondness for whiskey: "I had entered the place where I found Will Bill and two companions playing cards at a table for whisky. . . . Bill was a voracious drinker, and it was customary for him to say, upon being introduced to a stranger, 'Time to take a drink. It makes me [expletive] dry talking to you [expletive] [expletive] [expletive]." After Bill was murdered, Calamity left Deadwood, but she didn't leave her bad habits behind. In the 1880s she headed to Missoula County, Montana, where she was caught selling whiskey to the local Indians.[47]

She and Bill had downed plenty of whiskey during their Deadwood days, and Hickok's love of whiskey was captured in a newspaper, told by Captain Jack Crawford: "By the way, I heard a very funny story told on Bill some time ago. If you remember, he married Mrs. Agnes Lake, widow of Lake, the circus man. Bill fairly worshipped his wife, but despite his great love for her she never could induce him to quit drinking. He would come home full of bad whisky, and one day Mrs. Hickok said to him: 'Bill, if you don't quit drinking this pretty soon you will actually begin to see monkeys.' 'Monkeys?' said he. 'What do you mean, little one?'

'Why, you know, when the people back East drink too much of the kind of whiskey they get back there they see snakes, but this awful stiff out here makes them see monkeys.' Bill laughed at her and did not give the matter a second thought, little dreaming she had 'put up a job' to break him of his intemperance habits. There was a tame monkey in the town—Cheyenne, I believe it was—and Mrs. Hickok had induced its owner to loan it to her for a night. Bill came home that night comfortable drunk, and after he had gone to sleep his wife secured the monkey and chained [it] to the foot of the bed. Then turning down the light a little, she too retired and awaited the results. Bill woke up bleary-eyed to get some water and saw the monkey at the foot of his bed. He grabbed his revolver and leveled at the monkey and said, 'Now, old man, if you are a monkey you're in a bad fix; if you ain't a monkey I'm in a bad fix.' He shot the innocent monkey and said to Agnes, 'Little woman, congratulate me, for I have just had a wonderful escape. I ain't as drunk as I thought I was, and there is a monkey lyin' there on the floor that'll never intrude itself into the domestic felicity of another happy family an' make a gentleman think he's got the jim jams.'"[48]

As Deadwood's gold rush was in full swing, pioneers, miners, gamblers, and more were flush with Leadville fever. Gold was discovered early on, but the town boomed when silver and lead were discovered in the 1870s. From 1878 to 1879 the population hovered around six to eight thousand individuals. Reports filled the newspapers across America. The western papers compared each new boomtown to the last. A paper in Deer Lodge, Montana, noted that Leadville had claimed it was larger than Deadwood. In Leadville a hardworking miner earned three dollars per day, and he often spent it in a saloon or dance hall. Whiskey cost twenty-five cents per drink and was a lot cheaper than milk. Many saloons offered credit to their patrons who didn't have the funds to pay for their whiskey drinks. A term that was used to describe this practice was "jawbone whiskey." It meant that a man with no cash could verbally promise to settle up his bar tab when he got paid. The saloon owner kept a ledger and made a note of how much a patron owed him. The whiskey in Leadville was not the best, and a Kansas paper noted that it "is 90 degrees above the high-water mark." Another shot was taken at Leadville's whiskey by a St. Joseph, Missouri, newspaper: "Leadville whisky assays ninety-eight percent of pure spring water. That kind of beverage will strike with consternation the average stomach of the St. Joseph prospector."[49, 50, 51]

As Oscar Wilde traveled across the West in 1882, he ended up in Leadville. He penned, "From Salt Lake City one travels over the great plains of Colorado and up the Rocky Mountains, on the top of which is Leadville, the richest city in the world. It has also got the reputation of being the roughest, and every man carries a revolver. I was told that if I went there they would be sure to shoot me or my travelling manager. I wrote and told them that nothing they could do to my travelling manager would intimidate me. They are miners—men working in metals, so I lectured to them on the Ethics of Art. I read them passages from the autobiography of Benevento Cellini and they seemed much delighted. I was reproved by my hearers for not having brought him with me. I explained that he had been dead for some little time which elicited the enquiry 'Who shot him?' They afterwards took me to a dancing saloon where I saw the only rational method of art criticism I have ever come across. Over the piano was printed a notice: PLEASE DO NOT SHOOT THE PIANIST. HE IS DOING HIS BEST. The mortality among pianists in that place is marvelous. Then they asked me to supper, and having accepted, I had to descend a mine in a rickety bucket in which it was impossible to be graceful. Having got into the heart of the mountain I had supper, the first course being whisky, the second whisky and the third whisky. I went to the Theatre to lecture and I was informed that just before I went there two men had been seized for committing a murder, and in that theatre they had been brought on to the stage at eight o'clock in the evening, and then and there tried and executed before a crowded audience. But I found these miners very charming and not at all rough."[52]

Some miners from Leadville moved on to Tombstone, Arizona, when silver was discovered there. It started out in a remote region of southern Arizona where water and lumber were scarce, but it quickly turned into a town with miners, businessmen, gamblers, and cowboys. Rapidly exploding in population from its founding in 1879, the town quickly grew to be one of the most famous boomtowns in the history of the West. Like other towns, Tombstone had its share of fancy whiskey-drinking places. In fact, the saloons in this silver mining town flourished, and their sophistication and quantity reflected the town's boom. In 1881 there were about fifty saloons for the three thousand inhabitants to patronize. All sorts of business was conducted in these elegant edifices, including official US government business. Census taker Philip Thurmond set up a table in Comstock & Brown's saloon to make sure he reached the majority of men in town. Setting up a census table in a saloon was not a problem, since most stayed open all the time. Arizona pioneer Mrs. Hempe noted that, too. "Saloons and gambling places were always open, in fact the town never slept, it was full of life from day-break to day-break, and then some—a beehive of activity." During Tombstone's height in the mid-1880s, it cost about six dollars for a quarterly saloon business license. In addition to local taxes, saloon owners across the West were required, according to the Internal Revenue law, to purchase annual revenue licenses. Breweries, saloons, and tobacco shops had to have them as well. While the licenses were issued annually, they needed to be punched for each month they were used. An Internal Revenue collector visited the towns or local officials were made revenue officers. Attorney Wells Spicer acted as Tombstone's, and he was supplied with the necessary blank forms. Business owners who failed to get their licenses and pay their fees on time faced stiff penalties.

With their license and revenue forms secured, the Oriental Saloon opened with great fanfare. This detailed account of the Oriental Saloon in Tombstone provides an understanding of the sheer opulence of the places where whiskey was consumed. Milton Joyce & Co. opened its doors on July 21, 1880, and the *Tombstone Epitaph* reported that this "soon to be famous" saloon was the most elegantly furnished saloon "this side of the Golden Gate." The *Epitaph* reporter gave a detailed description of the saloon:

> *Twenty-eight burners suspended in neat chandeliers afforded*
> *an illumination of ample brilliancy, and the bright rays*

reflected from many colored crystals on the bar sparkled like a December iceling in the sunshine. The saloon comprised two apartments. To the right of the main entrance is the bar, beautifully carved, finished in white gilt and capped with a handsomely polished top. In the rear of this stand a brace of side-boards which are simply elegant and must be seen to be appreciated. They were made for the Baldwin Hotel, of San Francisco, but being too small, Mr. Joyce purchased them. The back apartment is covered with brilliant Brussels carpet, and suitably furnished after the style of a grand club room, with conveniences for the wily dealers in polished ivory. The selection of furniture and fixtures displays an exquisite taste, and nothing seems to have been forgotten—even a handsome stock of stationery.

Presiding over the bar was Johnny Chenowith. He didn't just offer Rock and Rye in a whiskey glass; he created wonderful specialty drinks like whiskey cocktails and Russian cocktails. The *Epitaph* reported: "If he can set up drinks as fast as his brother can score at a walking match, he will be an invaluable treasure to his employers." Patrons were serenaded by pianist Charley Willoughby, and caterer Isaac "Little Jakey" Jacobs provided patrons with delicious morsels. Jacobs provided the Oriental's customers with fresh oysters, shrimp, and crabs imported from San Francisco. The famous lawman Wyatt Earp even had a faro table in the Oriental during his stay in Tombstone in the 1880s. Saloons around the West served "free lunches" and salty snacks to paying customers. It not only enticed them in, but also made them thirsty. Saloons offered pickled herring, roast beef, roast turkey, pickled eggs, sardines and olives, sandwiches, and pretzels. Some even offered pâté de foie gras and caviar!

Tombstone's saloons were impressive, even for those who lived in larger cities in California. Newly relocated from San Diego to Tombstone, Clara Brown wrote, "Saloon openings are all the rage.

The Oriental is simply gorgeous and is pronounced the finest place of the kind this side of San Francisco. The bar is a marvel of beauty; the sideboards were made for the Baldwin Hotel; the gaming room connected is carpeted with Brussels; brilliantly lighted, and furnished with reading matter and writing materials for its patrons. Every evening music from the piano and violin attracts a crowd; and the scene is really a gay one—but for all the men."[53]

Whiskey, and bad whiskey at that, was the cause of the first disastrous fire that Tombstone experienced. June 22, 1881, began innocently enough, but the Arcade Saloon, owned by Mr. Alexander and Mr. Thompson, was about to make Tombstone history. With warm weather and a gentle, refreshing breeze, people moved about the day and tended to their normal duties until a loud clap of a thunderous nature interrupted them. It wasn't a storm though; it was an explosion. Mr. Alexander of the Arcade Saloon had finally decided to have a barrel of condemned whiskey shipped away. Before it could be shipped, however, he needed to measure the amount of liquor in the barrel. Using a gauge rod to measure the liquor, he accidentally dropped it into the barrel. His bartender, Mr. Hazelton, came out from behind the bar to retrieve the rod for him, carelessly bringing his lit cigar with him. Hazelton, for reasons unknown, also lit a match, and when the fumes from the liquor reached the open flame, there was an instantaneous explosion.[54]

Fortunately, no one in the saloon was injured, and everyone escaped through a back door. But in less than three minutes the flames had reached the attached buildings, and the town was being consumed in a fiery storm. People standing across the street from the saloon felt the blast, and some even sustained burns from the force of the explosion. The fire alarm was immediately sounded, but because of the lack of facilities for extinguishing the blaze, the fire grew out of control. When it was all over, Tombstone residents began clearing away the charred debris and put their town back together—whiskey be damned.

A comical story about an old tramp working a Tombstone bartender for free whiskey was so funny that the *Tombstone Epitaph* reported it. The story is from the Oriental Saloon, where an old man of about seventy years sat in the back of the saloon near the stove. He slowly worked his way to the bar and said to the barkeeper, "Boss, I think I'll go home, but I'd like a drop of the flush come-to-my-face-quick before I go." Since the barkeeper disliked tramps almost as much as he did old men, he obliged, settling on the lesser of the two evils. After the bartender set out the bottle, the old man took a drink that "would paralyze an army mule." He stood at the bar for a few minutes, and then made his way to the door.

A few minutes afterward and unbeknownst to the bartender, he returned to the saloon by way of its rear entrance. He took his previous seat by the stove and, after a short time, arose, turned up his collar, and pulled his hat over his eyes. He said to the barkeeper, "Well, I think I'll take a drink and go home; I feel somewhat exhausted from a long walk from Benson."

The barkeeper replied, "All right. Pass in your checks, and I'll give you your change."

"Well, my boy," said the tramp, "I'm an old man and a poor man and was in hopes you might give me a nightcap."

As the barkeeper placed the bottle on the bar, he said, "You look wonderfully like an old tramp I treated a few minutes ago."

The old codger replied, "Oh, no, I guess it was my brother." He took his drink and went on his way.

Just moments later the bartender noticed the old tramp back in his seat near the stove, except this time he was wearing an old handkerchief around his neck, his hat tipped to one side, and his coat lapels opened. As he sauntered to the bar for another free drink, the bartender said, "Now look here, my ancient sardine, I'm getting onto your little game, and it won't go. I've treated you twice within the last half an hour."

"Oh, no," replied the tramp, "I think it must have been my brother."

The barkeeper replied, "Well, just step outside and fetch them all in; I never hurt a man in my life, but I'll be damned if I wouldn't like to start in and make a clean sweep of a whole family." As he reached under the bar for his club, the old vagrant scooted out the door, perhaps to look for his "brother."

Coeur d'Alene, Idaho, was the next big mining boomtown, and one of its saloons made the newspapers all over the mining circuit. In 1883 the *Idaho Daily Statesman* wrote a story titled "The Coeur d'Alene Saloonist." It began: "Eagle City is located in the forks of Prichard and Eagle creeks. It has more saloons and faro games than you can shake a stick at. The stock in trade consists of a sack of flour for a bar, a bottle of coffin varnish, a bucket of water and two sized glasses. It is amusing to watch the strategic movements of the miners as they try to corral the big glass for their tansy, but the weather will have to be more tropical than it [is] now when they can elude the watchful eye of the 'barkeep.'"[55]

Mining strikes continued on the frontier, and Creede, Colorado, was the next big silver mining community to be put on the map. Nicholas Creede was the man who discovered silver in the Willow Creek district in 1890. While Creede may have found the silver, he was involved in a partnership that included George L. Smith and Charles H. Abbott. Smith and Abbott furnished the funds, while Creede did the searching. He named his first mine the Holy Moses. Newspaper accounts varied as to why he chose that name, but a biography about him published in 1894 explained how he settled on the name. The paper wrote, "Having driven a stake, Creede sat down to think of a name. There was little or nothing in a name, he thought, but he wanted to please his partner. He remembered that Smith had named three claims in Monarch, the 'Madonna,' the 'Cherubim,' and the 'Seraphim,' and he would follow in that line. Creede was not well versed in Biblical history, so knew very little of the saints and angels . . . he looked at the thick forest of pine that shaded the gentle slopes, and thought of the man who walked in the wilderness. And he called the mine the Moses; then fearing that his partner might object even to that, rubbed it out, and wrote 'Holy Moses.' The story of the new strike spread like a prairie fire."[56]

Creede's famous strike was made by Nicholas Creede, who named his first discovery the "Holy Moses." This saloon played off that name, and its owner later became the sheriff of Creede. Circa 1890s. DENVER PUBLIC LIBRARY

Once the news was out, prospectors and miners rushed to the area, and the town's population swelled to some ten thousand hopefuls. Entrepreneurial saloonkeepers, dance halls, and whiskey shops expanded to support the pioneers living in the area. In fact, there were sixty-five saloons, and one newspaper commented that "saloons do business night and day, every man is a walking arsenal and ready to 'shoot at the drop of a hat,' and reckless adventurers, regardless of human life, await the opportunity to better themselves . . . a missionary, Rev. Mr. Gaston, of Ouray, Colo., hoping to influence the spiritual life of the settlers, dropped into one of the principal saloons of Creede and asked permission to talk to the crowd for fifteen minutes. It was the largest barroom in the place and always crowded, but the faro dealers promptly vacated their chairs and the preacher mounted an improvised platform. Turning the leaves of the Bible, he took for his text, 'If a man dies shall he live again?' The 300 men within the sound of his voice promptly answered, 'Not in Creede.' The incident is homely, but it illustrates frontier life. A description of one of these mining camp saloons answers for all. It is about fifty feet long and say twenty feet wide, one story high, built of rough plank and run by two or three men, either one of whom is ready with Winchester or revolver to preserve peace."[57]

Even author Cy Warman noted how lively the town was and wrote a poem whose end was, "The cliffs are solid silver, With wondrous wealth untold; And the beds of the running rivers, Are lined with purest gold. While the world is filled with sorrow, And hearts must break and bleed, It's day all day in the day-time, And there is no night in Creede." The cost of living in Creede was said to be 50 percent higher than in other ordinary towns. "No fit meal" could be had for less than one dollar, a cot in a room with fifty to one hundred other cots cost from fifty cents to one dollar, and whiskey "that will not kill" cost at least twenty-five cents.[58, 59]

Many well-known characters made their way to Creede in pursuit of their fortune. Bob Ford, the outlaw known for killing Jesse James, was the town's first mayor and later operated a large saloon and gambling house. Early on, Ford and a man known as Joe Palmer decided to "paint the town red" after drinking too much Creede whiskey. They stood at the head of Creede Avenue and began firing their guns down the street and into businesses. They soon decided to head to nearby Cripple Creek to avoid any punishment. Ford later returned with the assistance of Soapy Smith.

Jefferson "Jeff" Randolph "Soapy" Smith, another character who was familiar to the people in Creede, took over after Ford was removed from office. One paper noted that "it was but a short time until he [Ford] was removed and another gambler known as 'Soapy Smith' put into office. 'Soapy' still holds the town." He was a saloonkeeper, bunco man, and often ran the underworld of the towns where he resided. His saloon in Creede was called the Orleans and was considered the largest early on. It was in the section of town called Jimtown, which was a corruption of the word Gintown.[60, 61]

Jimtown was the source of a devastating fire that consumed Creede and led to over a million dollars' worth of loss. On June 5, 1892, an explosion of coal oil in Thompson and Co.'s wholesale liquor house exploded. Jerry Guion was a saloonkeeper who was credited as having the only coherent story, which was captured by a reporter the day of the fiery disaster. He told them he was awakened at 5:30 a.m. by his porter, who was having words with a party of drunkards who had spent the night at Ford's dance house. The porter left to resolve the issue and Guion began to fall back asleep when his porter came back in a frantic state. When Guion woke up again, he saw that his room was filled with smoke. He rushed out of the building in his underclothes and left behind his pants, which held $2,800 in gold in the pockets. He wasn't outside ten minutes before the flames shot through the roof and had spread through the district. It was reported that an effort was made to

Creede, Colorado, was originally a famous Ute hunting ground and later became a silver mining boomtown. Circa 1892. CREEDE HISTORICAL SOCIETY

save merchandise and groceries, but men lost their heads when they saw their whiskey supply about to go up. They raced to save kegs of beer, cases of wine, and casks of whiskey. Once the booty was saved, the men helped themselves and soaked their sorrows in free liquor. The barrels of whiskey that couldn't be saved were seen floating down the inky creek. The mayor eventually ordered all saloons to close, and the whiskey-drinking street wanderers were discouraged from inciting others to drink. Creede residents eventually rebuilt their town and life continued.[62]

As Creede was rebuilding from its devastating fire, the mines in Cripple Creek, Colorado, were booming. Gold had been found there in 1890 and 1891 by Bob Womack, and the town was just beginning to be established. Stories about how the town got its name include its discoverer, Bob Womack. One story claims that he dug a large number of holes around the grazing land of cattle and the animals fell in the holes and became crippled. The other is about ol' Bob himself falling and becoming a cripple. Either way, the first store was established by Peter Hettic, who showed up with a tent in May 1891. He stocked it with a wagonload of goods that took two days to arrive. On July 7 he had relocated his business to a log storehouse. At first there was no cash in town and everything was done on credit or with gold dust. Hettic's first supplies included cheese, bacon, tobacco, crackers, a barrel of bottled beer, and five gallons of "unclassified" whiskey.

Large-scale production in the Cripple Creek mines didn't take place until 1892, when they produced six hundred thousand dollars. The following year saw some five thousand people living in Cripple Creek, and the gold output was just over two million dollars. A newspaper man by the name of Thomas Barton worked for the *Kansas Atchison Globe*. He made a trip to Cripple Creek and reported that the town was bustling. His story appeared in various western papers where he noted that most of the businesses were small frame buildings that either housed saloons or gambling houses. He observed that groceries and goods sold at reasonable prices, but that beer and whiskey were at a premium. He reported, "Beer is sold at two glasses for a quarter; whisky, the same price. A gambler is as good as anybody in Cripple Creek and a saloon keeper better. The town, however, is not 'tough.' You do not see men in the streets carrying pistols, but gambling tables are wide open. Cripple Creek is in the same county (El Paso) with Colorado Springs, where no liquor can be sold."[63, 64]

While Bob Womack is credited with starting the rush for gold in Cripple Creek, it wasn't money or fame that drove his quest. Bob, like most miners, longed for the thrill of discovery and not the rewards. He was not the first prospector to sell his claim for next to nothing. According to some, Bob sold his claim for a bottle of whiskey. It's quite possible because Bob was an ardent drinker. It was reported that he even spent some time in the Keeley intoxication program. A story with a comical spin on this appeared in an 1896 newspaper with a headline that read, "He Was the Cripple: And It Was He Who Discovered Things at the Creek." The story continued:

> "Yes, I know all about Cripple Creek," said the man with the stiff knee as he bent down for a chew of a navy plug. "In fact, the place was named after me. I fell down on the banks of the creek and crippled myself. I was still limping around when I discovered the first mine."
>
> "So you discovered the first mine?" was asked.
>
> "I have the honor, sir. Yes, I discovered the first mine, and sold it for a gallon of whisky. Up to date over $2,000,000 had been taken out of that claim."
>
> "Pretty dear whisky, eh?"
>
> "Oh, well, I'm not kicking. It was good whisky—the best I ever saw out west. I made it last me two weeks, and after it was gone I went out and discovered the Princess mine. I had just staked my claim when a critter came along with four pounds of tobacco and we made the even exchange. The returns

from the Princess have been $300,000 a month for several years past."

"Wasn't that a pretty good price for tobacco?" asked the interviewer.

"Well, rather high, but I couldn't chaw roots, you know. I was on the last plug when I discovered the Little Daisy mine. She was the richest of all, and I meant to get a million dollars out of her or bust. I held on for two or three weeks. And then a feller came along with an old hoss and struck me for a dicker. I got the hoss and the revolver and he got the mine. She's estimated at $4,000,000 today."

"But why didn't you hold on to it?"

"Couldn't do it my friend, and keep my place in society. All the bon-ton were on hoss-back to chase Chinamen around, and I had to go with the swells or lose my reputation."[65]

By 1895 the amount of gold reached about eight million dollars. Because of its wealth, Cripple Creek was a modern city for its time, as it had running water with plumbing, electric lights, and a sewer system. It also had a telephone system, two daily newspapers, "palatial" hotels, bookstores, and dry good businesses that sold silk and linen. The restaurants served venison, lobster, pheasants, quail, fresh mushrooms, strawberries, and tomatoes. While some accounts made the city sound like a fine place to call home, others did not.[66]

A newspaper ran an in-your-face account of what it called the "wickedest town on this continent." The article stated that about ten western locales had worn that distinction over time. The bad men of Dodge City, Leadville, and Creede had left those towns when their boom was over and now Cripple Creek was their home. The paper reported, "But two years ago, brought such a combination of bravado, lack of conscience and general cussedness that in a very short time it earned a seat on the devil's right hand. To this influx of desperadoes is plainly traceable the great labor

Cripple Creek, Colorado, was one of the biggest gold mine boomtowns of the West at the end of the nineteenth century, and the Colorado Liquor House served the thirsty thousands. Note the ad in the window for "hot free lunch day & night." Circa 1890s. DENVER PUBLIC LIBRARY

strike of last year." Cripple Creek's whiskey stories are endless, but let's begin with Kid Williams, who was the son of a Missouri doctor. He once wandered into a saloon, kicked everyone out, and proceeded to empty enough whiskey into a wash pan so he could bathe in it. He was at least smart enough to close the doors, but he did not draw the curtains and was photographed by a local photographer. Because drinking at ten thousand feet elevation can have different effects than at lesser elevations, people often got drunker than they intended. A case in point was a young Cripple Creek attorney who drank too much "coffin varnish." He gallantly walked into a saloon with a stick of gunpowder in his mouth. He drew a match to light it and ended up having the saloon to himself. He was later fined fifteen dollars in court for his escapade.[67]

By 1896 the town was in full swing, and saloons and gambling places were still plentiful. Thirty thousand people called it home and could choose from approximately eighty saloons. Along the main business street, just about every other business was a saloon or gambling hall. Games ran the gamut—faro, roulette, poker, wheels of fortune, craps, and more. They operated twenty-four hours a day to accommodate the miners who worked eight hours on and eight hours off. Selling whiskey in one of these places was not cheap, costing six hundred dollars per year. The dance halls were found on "Easy Street" and there were about twelve of them. Everything appeared to be a normal saloon upon first entering, but after a patron entered the back door, he saw a large room, with loud music screeching. It was in here where men could be found both drunk and sober. The women were here for the men's pleasure and not their own. Some wore traditional Victorian clothing, while others were more scantily clad. One visitor stated, "The faces are all flush with drink, and some of the women almost stagger as they push their way in and out among the men, begging them to dance and drink with them. There is no charge for dancing, but the man who dances is expected to treat his partner, and the girls are held out as a bait to sell the liquor and to get the drunken miners to gamble."[68]

While Cripple Creek was booming, a new find got prospectors and businessmen alike excited. The Klondike and Yukon Rivers, bordering both Alaska and Canada, were the final frontier when it came to mining in the West. As early as 1895, hopeful fortune seekers were searching for gold on the Yukon River in Alaska and Canada. In the late 1890s, thousands departed California and Washington ports in search of gold in the Yukon Territory. Getting supplies to the Yukon was a challenge because of the steep and snowy terrain. The best way to get supplies and gear was to use the natural terrain as a toboggan slide. The town of Circle City was the nearest settlement to the mining district and contained about 125 dwellings, fifteen saloons, three stores, and an opera house. It was reported that the land "flowed with whiskey." Intrepid pioneers kept arriving in the territory despite the harsh conditions, and in November 1895 the Birch Creek mining district was expected to yield over four hundred thousand dollars in gold dust and nuggets by the following summer.

A Klondiker by the name of H. H. Paramore wrote a book called *The Practical Guide to America's New El Dorado: Klondike Gold Fields* in 1897. In it he recalled an incident where whiskey saved his friend's life after he was nearly killed sliding their gear down a hill. He wrote, "A mile a minute was nothing. They landed all safe, however, at the bottom on the Yukon side. Then we followed, sliding and tumbling after. In going down, however, one of my partners was nearly killed. Gibbons, who was half way down the mountain side, was struck by the last sleigh we let go and knocked about fifty feet. I thought we would have to bury him there where we picked him up, but he was simply stunned, and after half hour's rubbing and frequent doses of whisky he revived and was able to continue the journey." While Paramore's partners headed to Circle City, he stayed at the Klondike gold fields, where he got his first job working in a saloon. He created poker, faro, and crap tables and in return received fifteen dollars per day, which included his meals. His salary was slightly higher due to demand than similar workers in Circle City, where wages were ten to twelve dollars per day. He ended up selling his extra provisions and struck gold with his enterprise, even if he didn't find any actual nuggets. He recalled, "I sold one gallon of whisky that cost me, in Seattle, $8, for $25. Bacon that cost me 11 c. I sold for 75c per pound. I sold a 150-pound sack of flour for $30; tea that cost me 25c per pound for $2 per pound. Sugar I sold for 60c per pound. One suit of underwear I sold for $12." He also recalled how some pioneers felt about regulating the whiskey trade: "Mr. Ogilvie takes up the subject of the liquor traffic also, saying: 'The impression of the best men here, saloon men and all, is that the liquor trade should be regulated and no one but responsible parties should be allowed to bring liquor in. Now, any loafer who can gather enough money to secure a few gallons and a few glasses and wants to have an idle time, sets up a saloon.'"[69, 70]

It wasn't until 1897, when a ship laden with gold from the Yukon arrived in San Francisco, that the stampede began. Many made the trek from Tacoma, Washington, via Chilkoot Pass, which was the most popular but also the steepest route to the gold fields. Dawson City was one of the liveliest of the Yukon gold rush towns at this time. The bustling city was located in the Yukon, and the Klondike River ran right through it. New arrivals would have seen over eighty log cabins and some six hundred tents when they arrived, and in November 1897 between twenty-five hundred and three thousand pioneers called it home. Even though the largest population was made up of male miners, several families and about thirty children lived there. Two or three saloons offered "the poorest kind of whiskey" for fifty cents per glass. It was reported that the principal business engaged in was the sale of intoxicants. Men were told to plan on spending three hundred to one thousand dollars per day for three square meals. That may seem exorbitant, but many miners spent hours in the gulches toiling for gold nuggets and then turned right around and spent thousands of dollars' worth of gold nuggets at one of the many gambling outfits. The *Beeville Bee* reported about such an incident: "Behind every bar are tin cans, cups, and beer glasses containing pounds of yellow metal fresh from the mines. Men come in from the diggings and take their places at the gambling tables with the ease and nonchalance of millionaire gamblers. Tonight 'Swift Water Bill,' who owns one of the richest claims on El Dorado Creek, came to town and took a seat at the faro table. In an hour, he had lost $7500 in gold nuggets. Arising from the table he lighted his cigar and invited the house to drink at his expense. The treat cost him $112." Because the gold fields were partly on US land and partly on Canadian soil, businessmen were often subject to laws and taxes from both governments. In December 1897 the Canadian

government decided to apply a two dollar per gallon tax on whiskey to try and stop the flow of whiskey into the Klondike region.
A newspaper commented, "With whiskey selling at 50 cents a
drink, or $10 a bottle, as it was according to the latest reports, the
sellers can afford to pay a heavy tax."[71, 72]

Whiskey was in high demand in many of the towns that sprang
up to support the Yukon Territory gold rush. The men who
flooded into St. Michael, Weare, Rampart, Fort Yukon, Circle
City, and Eagle City were all in want of one thing—whiskey, and
gold, of course. In late 1898 a whiskey shipment of one thousand
gallons was anticipated from a whiskey syndicate that included
John Malone, Joe Harvey, Billy Darmer, and Dave Argyle for
many Yukon towns. Charles Wilson and former lawman Wyatt
Earp were running Malone's gambling and liquor house in
Rampart and were expecting a portion of this shipment, but
Malone ran into trouble when he tried to have it shipped.
Malone thought he had secured all the proper paperwork he
needed, which was a permit from the governor for the whiskey
to be used for medicinal purposes. But federal officers failed to
give Malone a whiskey landing permit when they arrived at St.
Michael. Officials at St. Michael seized the cargo and shipped it
back to Tacoma, Washington.[73]

By 1899 a whiskey monopoly set the price and availability of
the golden elixir in the Yukon Territory. In midwinter whiskey
was selling at ten dollars per gallon, but by June it had skyrock-
eted to thirty-two dollars. A group of men formed the North
American Transportation and Trading Company and cornered
the "booze" market. It was reported that the company's liquor
rooms held 100,000 to 150,000 gallons of various grades of
whiskey. Only small amounts of whiskey could be found in other
houses or saloons, and shipments were being stopped. Alexander
McDonald, who was called the "Scotch Temperance King of the

Klondike," was waiting on a shipment of 40,000 gallons, but it was stalled near Bennett City. A newspaper reported, "There are millions in the scheme for both the company and the government, and the miner will have to pay for it."[74]

Because of the whiskey monopoly, the cost of whiskey shot up in Dawson City. In 1899 the *River Press* in Fort Benton, Montana, reported, "Whiskey sells in Dawson City for $1 per glass, and sometimes it isn't whiskey either. In the matter of expense a high old time in that town is precisely what the term implies."[75]

The next big strike in Alaska proper was the Nome gold rush, which happened with the Discovery Claim on Anvil Creek, E.O. Lindblom Placer Claim, and No. 1 on Snow Creek Placer Claim. Cape Nome sprang up to support the mines on the Snake River in 1898. One report noted that saloons and gambling houses were making "bushels" of money. Whiskey was selling at fifty cents per drink and from three to five dollars per bottle. A newspaper reported, "A supply of whisky in this country means a fortune. I have never seen anything like it. If you had a saloon in the Cape Nome country you could retire in two years with a fortune to look after."[76]

Wyatt Earp was one of those men who ran a saloon in Nome from 1898 to 1899. He and his partner, Charley Hoxie, ran the Dexter saloon, and Wyatt also had a land office. They did a brisk business in Nome, and he said of his then home, "I have followed every mining excitement for thirty years and seen the biggest, but Nome 'lays over' all the others. It has the advantages of all, without any of the disadvantages."[77]

Another intrepid Nome resident was Lanier McKee, who penned a book called *The Land of Nome: A Narrative Sketch of the Rush to Our Bering Sea Gold-Fields*. In it he described how Nome's gold rush began:

> *The remarkable discoveries of gold at Cape Nome, Alaska, situated almost in the Bering Strait, only one hundred and fifty miles from Siberia, and distant not less than three thousand*

Alaska was the last hurrah for mining on the frontier. Fortune seekers from miners to saloon men rushed to experience the Klondike gold rush. As many as a hundred thousand prospectors made their way up Chilkoot Pass to the Yukon Territory between 1896 and 1900. Circa 1899. LIBRARY OF CONGRESS

miles from San Francisco and fifteen hundred from the famed Klondike, naturally created more excitement in the Western and mining sections of this country than in the Middle States and the "effete East," an expression frequently heard in the West. These rich placer-gold deposits were discovered by a small party of prospectors in the late autumn of 1898. The news spread like fire consumes dead timber from the Pacific coast and up into Dawson and the Klondike country. The following spring witnessed a stampede to the new El Dorado, which, however, was wholly eclipsed by the unprecedented mad rush of eighteen thousand persons in the spring ensuing. During the summer months of 1899, when, in addition to the gold along the creeks, rich deposits, easy to extract, were found in the beach extending for miles by the sea, everyone at Nome had an opportunity to share in nature's unexpected gift.

McKee described the saloons in Nome: "The saloon which bore the proud sign 'The Only Second-Class Saloon in Alaska' seemed to be the best appointed and to be playing to the largest audiences; but it was then too early for the miners to come in with their gold dust, and the gamblers, therefore, were not doing a harvest business." Of whiskey, he recalled a couple of stories. "It was difficult to locate one's self, sitting or standing, so as to avoid a trickle of water down the neck. Here was a good time for a bottle of whisky to get in its work, and Louis needed a stiff drink, for he was pretty ill. So, round it went throughout the choice circle, and back it came to me, empty enough. . . . Ripley and whisky, I was informed, were always associated together—were almost synonymous terms—and whenever 'Joe' struck town it was a gala day for the saloons."[78]

Wearing a parka of reindeer skin, reindeer fur boots, and a fur cap, LaBelle Brooks-Vincent took a dogsled team to Dawson and then to Nome after she was lured into a mining claim scheme. She was a determined and a somewhat trusting single woman who lived on pilot bread and drank her tea from a tin can until she was able to get some of her supplies back and settle into her life amid the men. She wrote a book about the gold rush, but her work also included many of the things that were rarely written about. She titled her book *The Scarlet Life of Dawson and the Roseate Dawn of Nome*. She recalled the dark life of cheating, suicides, prostitution, abuse, death, and more. Her accounts of whiskey and its business offer a different perspective than those of most of the male pioneers who trekked into the Yukon. In one account she recalled the use of *hooch*, a slang word used today for whiskey. Hooch was a common word used during the gold rushes in Alaska and was originated by the Hoochino Indians of Alaska that meant strong or illegally produced liquor. Brooks-Vincent wrote in 1900, "In Alaska a truce exists between real and the bogus authority in the sale of whiskey, by means of bribery and a regular tax of a dollar per gallon. This is usually admitted. The manufacture of 'Hootch,' an intoxicating beverage, is also a hidden spring of the Scarlet Life. Some men of high social standing have made practical use of their knowledge of alchemy in this direction. The magical properties of Hootch are unique, and are sufficient to transform a poor miner into a millionaire for the time being, and also to make a millionaire miner a poor man. It is the 'claim' of the knowing saloon-keeper, who prefers not to work, but to linger near a warm fire in winter while the miners work. He knows that at the clean-up the miners will salt his claim with genuine gold, and the precious metal which shone with promise between the riffles in the sluice-box, will lie darkly under cover in his capacious sack. Miners' meetings are sometimes dry when the favored contestant is privileged to furnish to the judge and jury the liquid stimulant necessary to a decision in his favor." She also noted that anyone with some knowledge of mining stampedes was going to Nome to sell whiskey and manage dance halls and gambling houses.[79]

The Yukon Territory was the final frontier of the American West. After the turn of the twentieth century, the western landscape was no longer wild and untamed. Pioneers had populated many locales across the country, and new towns, counties, and states were created. Enforced laws, churches, schools, temperance movements, and all the things that come with organized society were redefining the landscape of the West. As the West was tamed, the same influences sought to regulate the whiskey industry. The association between whiskey and the western saloon had been solidified. Whiskey helped create the West, and it will forever be tied to its past, present, and, likely, its future.

Chapter Six

The Iron Horse: How It Connected the West

During the early part of the nineteenth century, whiskey was shipped to the far reaches of North America in barrels from eastern and midwestern distillers via ships, overland wagons, and limited-track railroads. Expansion of the iron horse was good for business, travel, and commerce, and almost immediately, sleepy towns were transformed into bustling cities with depots, railroad workers, freighters, and a burst of vice-related elements.

This train depot in Idaho shows barrels on the loading dock awaiting rail transportation. Circa 1800s. UTAH STATE HISTORICAL SOCIETY

When it was founded in 1860, Sedalia, Missouri, had no railroad and the nearest railroad terminus was in Tipton, some twenty-five miles away. It got closer when it reached Syracuse at twenty miles, and even closer at thirteen miles from Otterville. It inched even closer when it came to Smithton, which was just about nine miles distant. When at last the tracks made their way to Sedalia, residents were excited about having the railroad come to their town, but they soon learned what came along with that. When towns were the termini, they were crowded with freighters of every description eager to pick up some of the large quantity of goods brought by the rails and to distribute the goods to nearby towns that had no railroad. As the railroads abandoned one town for another, businesses shifted. A resident of Sedalia remembered the arrival of the Missouri Pacific Railroad:

> *When the railroad reached Sedalia, those who lived in this vicinity, and still live here, can remember that there was a genuine rush for Sedalia, like that made for some rich mining district in the far west. The name of the town was attractive in sound, and novel as well, in a region filled with towns with old, staid, practical, every day names. The novelty and euphony of the name seemed to be significant of a new era in Central Missouri, and it has proven so. The large stores and establishments at Otterville and Syracuse were moved to Sedalia, not only the stocks, but in many cases the buildings or portions of them, or the timber. Houses and portions of them were brought from Georgetown on wagons, and just as soon as a man could get anything to protect goods, that would pass muster for a house, he began business. Just before the railroad got to Sedalia, the supplies for the Southwest Expedition, which was an expedition to the Kansas border, were brought by rail to Smithton. That was about the last time that it had, what would be called in the expressive slang of the present day, "a business boom." As soon as the railroad reached Sedalia, it became at once the depot*

of the Overland Stage Line and the headquarters for supplies,
as the other towns where the line had paused for a time had
been. Here, in a few weeks after the railroad had reached the
point, the trains of wagons loaded. Just when the excitement
and rush was at its height, war was declared. In one respect
this was a misfortune to them; in another, it was an immense
advantage. It delayed the active and vigorous work of building
the town for the four years that the war continued. On the
other hand, it held at the place the terminus of the railroad for
nearly three years. . . . It was then "the Bullwhacker," the indi-
vidual who drove the six yoke of oxen attached to an enormous
wagon for the transportation of goods to the southwest, was in
his full glory; the broad-rimmed, slouched hat was the popular
head covering, bread and bacon the favorite diet, and whisky
and New Orleans molasses mixed, the only drink that men of
mettle would touch. A revolver in those days was as sure to be
found on a man's person as a lead pencil and a memorandum
book are now-a-days.

Sedalia continued to grow and thrive, although one day it was
noted as being peculiarly "dull." The *Sedalia Weekly Bazoo* reported,
"It has been a dull day. A very dull day. The sky was dark with a
cold, damp fog. . . . Even whisky lost its vigor, and fell into the glass
from the decanter without a sparkle or bead, while the billiard ball
lazily crawled across the cloth on its hands and knees."[1]

Even though rails were reaching places like Sedalia, none yet
connected from coast to coast. The push to connect the coasts of
America was made possible when President Lincoln signed the
Pacific Railroad Act of 1862. This act of Congress chartered two
railroad corporations to build the line: The Union Pacific was to
build westward from the Missouri River and the Central Pacific
was to build eastward from Sacramento, California. The Central
Pacific was at that time a limited route, traveling from Sacramento
to the Sierra Nevada.

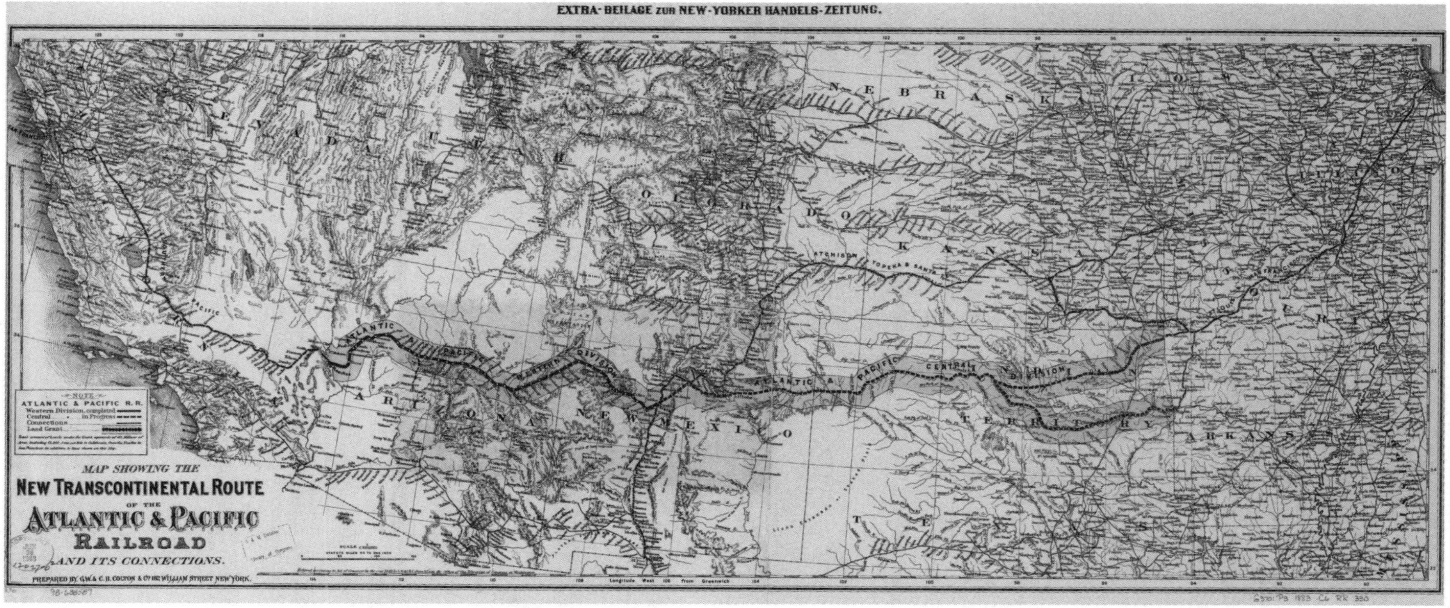

MAP SHOWING THE
NEW TRANSCONTINENTAL ROUTE
of the
ATLANTIC & PACIFIC
RAILROAD
AND ITS CONNECTIONS.

Map showing the new transcontinental route of the Atlantic & Pacific Railroad and its connections in 1883. LIBRARY OF CONGRESS, MAP COLLECTIONS

The Central Pacific Railroad broke ground first at Front and K Streets in Sacramento on January 8, 1863. Almost a year later, on December 2, the Union Pacific began work in Omaha, Nebraska. In 1865 the railroad laid a mere 40 miles of track, but in 1867 it made rapid progress and laid over 200 miles. The following year it only managed to get another 20 miles, but they had to traverse the ascent of the Rocky Mountains. From 1868 until the Union Pacific met the Central Pacific in 1869, it laid over 180 miles, not including the temporary lines that were used to complete the permanent ones.[2]

The railroads needed pure sweat and grit to get their tracks laid, and men from different ethnic backgrounds signed on for the

An 1868 photo of the Central Pacific Railroad near the Humboldt River Canyon in Nevada, showing barrels in the foreground of a makeshift and transient rail town campsite. NATIONAL ARCHIVES

job. The Central Pacific and Union Pacific primarily used Chinese and Irish workers; however, any man needing an income could be found along the railroad lines. Because laying track meant moving as the rails were laid, the workers and their families were akin to nomads in the desert. Once a few miles of track were laid, they would pack up their transportable homes and goods and set up at the next location, which was several miles ahead of where the next terminal town was projected. The railroads called them bases or terminal towns, but because of the harsh conditions and the crowds that followed this circuit, these towns were often referred to as "Hell on Wheels." Some of these towns included Fremont, Fort Kearney, and North Platte in Nebraska; Julesburg in Colorado; Cheyenne, Laramie, Benton, and Green River in Wyoming; and Evanston and Corrine in Utah. One newspaper captured the image of those towns: "Unknown, too, is that peculiarity of railroad construction in the Rocky Mountain region of the United States generally spoken of as 'Hell on Wheels' where the temporary termini of the road, as it progresses, are only a succession of shanties, whiskey dens, gambling holes, of license, robbery, riot and murder. In any of the rude frontier towns along this road in the Northwest Territory a lady can walk alone without the slightest molestation or insult."[3]

Samuel Bowles was one of the many men who toiled on the railroads and knew all too well about the evils of Hell on Wheels towns through his experience living in some during the summers of 1865 and 1866. He also noted the importance and benefit of the end result. In his book he stated,

> So completely is the Pacific Railroad henceforth the key to all our New West; so thoroughly must all knowledge of the characteristics of the latter radiate out from the former as a central line, that its story should be told almost at the outset, even to the anticipation of earlier experiences. Marked, indeed, was the contrast between the stage ride of 1865 and

the Railroad ride of 1868 across the Plains. The then long-drawn, tedious endurance of six days and nights, running the gauntlet of hostile Indians, was now accomplished in a single twenty-four hours, safe in a swiftly-moving train, and in a car that was an elegant drawing-room by day and a luxurious bedroom at night.

Regarding the towns called Hell on Wheels, he remarked,

As the Railroad marched thus rapidly across the broad Continent of plain and mountain, there was improvised a rough and temporary town at its every public stopping-place. As this was changed every thirty or forty days, these settlements were of the most perishable materials—canvas tents, plain board shanties, and turf-hovels—pulled down and sent forward for a new career, or deserted as worthless, at every grand movement of the Railroad company. Only a small proportion of their populations had aught to do with the road, or any legitimate occupation. Most were the hangers-on around the disbursements of such a gigantic work, catching the drippings from the feast in any and every form that it was possible to reach them. Restaurant and saloon keepers, gamblers, desperadoes of every grade, the vilest of men and of women made up this "Hell on Wheels," as it was most aptly termed.[4]

The chief engineer of the Union Pacific Railroad, Major General Grenville Dodge, painted a different picture of Hell on Wheels towns. He was trying to lure hopeful landowners to the areas where the railroad passed through, since the railroad was selling land and did not want to scare people away with stories of drunken railroad workers. In Julesburg, Colorado, he advertised lots selling from $50 to $250 each. He wrote of the firm that did most of the rail building: "Their force consisted of 100 teams and 1,000 men, living at the end of the track in boarding cars

Union Pacific construction employees wait for their payroll, which usually was spent on whiskey in the town's saloons. Circa 1800s. UTAH STATE HISTORICAL SOCIETY

and tents, and moved forward with it every few days. It was the best organized, best equipped and best disciplined track force I have ever seen. I think every chief of the different units of the force had been an officer of the army, and entered on this work the moment they were mustered out. They could lay from one to three miles of track per day, as they had material, and one day laid eight and a half miles. Their rapidity in track laying, as far as I know, has never been excelled. . . . Bases were organized for the delivery of material generally from one to two hundred miles apart, according to the facilities for operation. These bases were as follows: First, Fremont; second, Fort Kearney; third, North Platte; fourth, Julesburg; fifth, Sidney; sixth, Cheyenne; seventh, Laramie; eighth, Benton (the last crossing of the North Platte); ninth, Green River; tenth, Evanston; eleventh, Ogden, and finally Promontory [Corrine]. I have seen these terminal towns starting first with a few hundred people until at Cheyenne, at the base of the mountains, where we wintered in 1867–68, there were 10,000 people. From that point they decreased until at Green River there were not over 1,000. After we crossed the first range of mountains we moved our bases so rapidly they could not afford to move with us."[5]

Louisville, Kentucky, newspaper reporter D. R. Adonis wrote of the conditions at the beginning of the line in Omaha, Nebraska, and was more realistic. His story appeared in the *Denver Gazette* and was published in multiple western papers. Adonis also noted the conditions of the railroad town. He reported, "Since leaving 'Hell's Roost'—Omaha—up to my arrival at Denver, 10 o'clock a.m., I have not heard the crack of a pistol, nor even had the ever-welcome sight (to a newspaper man) of witnessing a free fight. The only dangerous weapons to a permanent peace between all parties I saw used were several hundred potations of villainous 'forty rod' rot gut whiskey."[6]

It's not surprising that whiskey and alcohol flowed freely in the Hell on Wheel towns because the water was anything but potable. The *Frontier Index* reported, "BAD WATER. The great cry here is, bad water, bad water. . . . " They also reported that water was selling for twenty-five cents per glass. Each town was well equipped with supplies because the railroad could move back and forth between Omaha, Nebraska, where wholesale goods were plentiful, to the end of the line. Not everyone could afford prime whiskey, which is why men like reporter Adonis recalled the rotgut.[7]

Fort Kearny, in Nebraska, was established in 1848 by the US Army along the Oregon Trail to offer protection from the threat of Indian attacks. The post was strategically located at a crossroads where several eastern trails merged and was on the bank of the Platte River. In 1866 it became the base for the Union Pacific Railroad. A small semiweekly paper called the *Herald* was started in early 1866, and the *Weekly Champion and Press* in Atchison, Kansas, wrote about the *Herald*, "It is an interesting little sheet, full of life and spirit." That paper became the *Frontier Index*, and its owner, Legh Freeman, followed the progress of the Union Pacific Railroad until the end. It was dubbed, "The Newspaper on Wheels," and could be found at the end of the line and sometimes farther out, waiting for the Union Pacific to arrive.[8]

A newspaper correspondent from New York wrote about his journey along the new Union Pacific from Omaha to North Platte in June 1867, where the tracks had stopped. Along the way, he observed the flatness of the land, the alkali water, and the emptiness of it all. He reported, "There are but few settlers on the line of the road. . . . Here and there are miserable adobe shanties, with signs out offering whisky and other luxuries to the weary sojourner, but I have not seen so much as the sign of a farm, or a gold, or even a patch for fully 100 miles." A year later North Platte received another bad report from the *Cheyenne Leader* in July. While the railroad had moved on, the wake of their Hell on Wheels lifestyle remained. They reported, "The railroad company has sunk a well to the depth of 27 feet in the new town, from which a mixture of mud, water, Epsom salts and alkali have been obtained, half a glass of which is a physic of the strongest quality. Fights are plenty, and generally free. Shooting commences on unsettled accounts of from 75 cents to $1.25. There is more whisky walking about in that community than in any other of the same size in the world." One year after North Platte was a booming terminal town, it was suffering from a lack of business. The *Frontier Index* ran this story: "North Platte. June 12, 1868. I landed here last Tuesday. Business is very dull; I have only seen two dollars change hands since I have been here. . . . At auction today, can goods were selling at 35 cents per can . . . whiskey from $1.50 to $3 per gallon; nails no sale. . . . H. C. Overbaker."[9, 10, 11]

Some businessmen knew the value of serving good whiskey and let their customers know it. An ad appeared in the *Commercial*

Record on April 4, 1868, in Cheyenne. It read, "Joe Venine, at the Keg House, next to Ware & Co's bank, is now prepared to furnish liquors direct from St. Louis to parties fitting out for Sweetwater. Any one wanting a good whiskey, should call and draw a glass from the original wood."[12]

The newspaper on wheels, the *Frontier Index*, knew the importance of the whiskey business to tax revenues. It ran a story on the whiskey tax that was being negotiated in Washington, DC, by the Ways and Means Committee. The article reported that delegates from Kentucky, Ohio, Illinois, and Indiana were present to urge the committee to reduce the tax on whiskey to fifty cents, down from sixty cents. It claimed that by reducing the tax the government would receive more revenue from those states alone for three months versus what had already been received for the whole country. It further argued that by doing this, it would be nearly impossible for illegal distillers to stay in business. Additionally, the article claimed that if the tax was reduced the government would almost immediately gain forty million dollars in taxes from the whiskey being held back from the market by those who could not compete with the illegal distillers who were defrauding the government of the tax.[13]

Farther down the line was Fort Sanders, Wyoming, which was built in July 1866 to provide safety and support for early Overland Trail emigrants; in 1868 it served as a base location for the Union Pacific Railroad until the town of Laramie, in what is now Wyoming, was established. The *Frontier Index* reported from Laramie on April 21: "We have it—Laramie City; it has just jumped into existence." When the railroad track laying settled here, the terminal (or termini, as they were often referred to) town afforded thirsty workers several locations to purchase liquor, including Liddell, Robertson & Brown's Outfitting Emporium, which was based out of Cheyenne and advertised that it was at the end of the track. Others were Lowry, Beall & Co., John Wanless & Co., and Harmon & Goodrich, which offered a large variety of supplies including canned goods, windows, nails, tobacco, and seventy barrels of whiskey. The *Frontier Index* reported on another saloon in town: "When any of our friends want a first-class drink of any kind, don't forget to call on Tommy Dillon at his new and spacious tent just above Crisman's building. He keeps the best of everything to drink and smoke, besides having the best band of music in the city." Sanders Dining Hall didn't receive quite the same endorsement, but the *Index* noted it served oysters: fresh, raw, stewed, and fried for those in need of a meal. Another restaurant, called the Tin, was opened by Smith & Wheeler and served meals at all hours of the day and night. In July 1868 editor Legh Freeman of the *Frontier Index* settled into his "new office" at Laramie, Wyoming. He went on a rant about how easterners talk bad about the termini towns. A reporter from back East was treated to a free ride on the Union Pacific, and when he returned he wrote,

> *Vice stalks its streets in daylight and revels in numerous haunts of dissipation when night adds horror to heart-sickening scenes of debauchery and licentiousness. Laramie has more dance houses, of the "genus" vile than has Chicago. Every night these dens, which combine the occupations of rum-sellers, gamblers, and harlots, are thrown open, and are patronized.*[14]

Freeman decided to print his stance on why those frightening stories were being taken back East. Not only did it appear in his paper, but some of the papers back East reprinted his story. He reported about a man who said less than favorable things about his current location after imbibing too much,

> *It is certainly amusing to read accounts of Laramie City, written by excursionists and correspondents after their return to the East. These unsophisticated, flannel mouth devils, when*

they come here think they know it all . . . but they invariable
go away, after having "danced to the tune of three or four hun-
dred dollars," very wise. They are never satisfied with losing
a hundred or two at faro or three card monte, but must visit
some of the dance houses and squander as much more in treat-
ing the "fair and frail" girls to wine and whisky, and other
such beastly fodder; and when they return to their senses and
find out how nicely they were inveigled, while intoxicated,
their indigitation knows no bounds—hence the terrible name
they give our city.[15]

In August 1868 Legh Freeman and his *Frontier Index* packed
up from Laramie and boarded the train to the next Hell on
Wheels town of Green River, Wyoming Territory, where he set
up his newspaper headquarters. Freeman reported on his journey:
"At Benton we debarked again and barked in the Caboose for
the night. Next morning our gaze was greeted with the sight of
some two hundred framed tents and portable buildings. . . . There
are perhaps, three thousand people in and around Benton and
many trains outfitting for Green River." As with the other Hell
on Wheels towns, goods were in short supply in the beginning.
Despite a plea from editor Freeman in mid-August for supplies,
his paper had numerous ads for them. Saloons included Fat Jack's,
the National Club, Jimmy Brown's Bank Exchange, Ed Harvey's,
J. Dailey's, Jenk's House Hotel bar, and Johnny Kingston's Who
Would A' Thought It Dance Hall. Places to dine included the
City Bakery, Fashion restaurant, Kalamazoo Lunch House, Lyon's,
Casement Chop House, and Goldstein's U.S. Restaurant, which
offered "the best the market can afford" and the "best liquors and
cigars." Several other people also sold whiskey and liquor, includ-
ing Green River local J. A. Gaston and M. M. Smith, who had
his main wholesaling operation back in Omaha. He advertised,
"Bourbon, rye, and Irish Whisky. Proprietor and manufacturer of
Four Ace Hard to Beat Whisky. Orders promptly attended to."

The stark contrast of Citadel Rock against the uncharted western land-scape shows the inception of the rail town's growth in Green River, Wyoming, 1868. LIBRARY OF CONGRESS

Kingston's Dance Hall was another enterprise offering libation and entertainment—prizefights and clog dancing were standard fare.

Benton Hell on Wheels worker Samuel Bowles's recollection of the businesses that advertised in the *Frontier Index* goes deeper than superficial newspaper print:

> *When we were on the line, this congregation of scum and wick-edness was within the Desert section, and was called Benton. One to two thousand men, and a dozen or two women were encamped on the alkali plain in tents and board shanties; not a tree, not a shrub, not a blade of grass was visible; the dust ankle deep as we walked through it, and so fine and volatile that the slightest breeze loaded the air with it, irritating every sense and poisoning half of them; a village of a few variety stores and shops, and many restaurants and grog-shops; by day*

disgusting, by night dangerous; almost everybody dirty, many
filthy, and with the marks of lowest vice; averaging a murder
a day; gambling and drinking, hurdy-gurdy dancing and the
vilest of sexual commerce, the chief business and pastime of
the hours,—this was Benton. Like its predecessors, it fairly
festered in corruption, disorder and death, and would have
rotted, even in this dry air, had it outlasted a brief sixty-day
life. But in a few weeks its tents were struck, its shanties
razed, and with their dwellers moved on fifty or a hundred
miles farther to repeat their life for another brief day. Where
these people came from originally; where they went to when
the road was finished, and their occupation was over, were
both puzzles too intricate for me. Hell would appear to have
been raked to furnish them; and to it they must have naturally
returned after graduating here, fitted for its highest seats and
most diabolical service.[16]

The Union Pacific reached Bear River City, just south of
Evanston, Wyoming, in the fall of 1868. Reports from this
terminal were pretty much the same as the previous ones from
the Hell on Wheels towns, and on October 23 bad whiskey
caused many enjoying a meal at the Southern Restaurant to
forget about their beef and coffee. The *Frontier Index* reported,
"Last Friday night somebody went crazy from the effects of
bad whisky and opened a promiscuous fire from a pistol, in the
Southern Restaurant, on Uintah street. It was not ascertained
what individual fired the shots, but Mike Ryan, Tom Tunsell,
Tom Taylor, and John Harrigan were all severally shot in the
legs. They are, however, all steadily improving." Bear River City
was one of the most violent of the Hell on Wheels towns, and in
early November 1868 the *Frontier Index* reported another incident: "On last Tuesday night, Jno. A. Hoffman was garroted near
the Railroad crossing of Utah street, and robbed of seventy-five
dollars. One ruffian choked him while another rifled his pockets.

John says they did not get all he had, and would not have gotten any if one of the policemen had not taken his revolver early in the evening, while in a state of intoxication. This is a bad country for a man to drink in, until he has to be deprived of defensive weapons, especially if he displays many greenbacks about the saloons." Ruffians ran the town, and on November 3, 1868, vigilantes broke into the jail to capture and lynch three "garroters." A riot broke out, and the police holed up in a store for safety as a mob burned the jail and the newspaper office of the *Frontier Index*. Newspaper editor Legh Freeman fled the town for Fort Bridger, but quickly returned to report the news. Twenty-five of the rioters died in the foray and another fifty or sixty were wounded. The *Frontier Index* reported on the importance of having a weapon while in Bear River City in January 1869, so "that honest men can walk the streets of the city now with safety, provided they keep sober and are armed to the teeth."[17, 18]

Bear River City, Wyoming, Police Report

November 10, 1868
    "The following named individuals who poured down too much 'mountain fire' to keep the cold out were arrested for being drunk and disorderly:

Chas. King, $5 and costs.
Pete Anderson, $5 and costs.
John Rice was fined $5 for costs, but failing to come down with the Lincoln skins [money], went to work on the streets.
E. P. Craven craved much drink and was mulcted [fined] in the sum of $10 and costs.
James Smith, $5 and costs.
A. Moore worked out a $10 fine on the streets.
Joe Kelly paid $10. J. Bronk, do [ditto].

J. Connors $5. Wm. Wolfers $15.
Chas. Noble, Mike Sweeney, Jno. McCarty,
Mike Noonan, $5 each.
John Lynch, $10.
P. Anderson having no money was set at work
on the streets.

Source: *Frontier Index*, November 10, 1868

On May 10, 1869, the American West was connected to the rest of the country when the Union and Central Pacific Railroads joined their tracks at Promontory Summit in Corrine, Utah Territory. Mrs. Mary Mathews Tolman's father was there, and she recalled, "My father was just a boy when the Union Pacific was being built but he and his father worked along the new road, mostly putting down wells. Father's name was John S. Mathews. The camps they lived in were very rough and not very good environment for a young boy, but then boys were pretty rugged and able to take care of themselves, better than they could, perhaps do, today. I really know very little of their experiences along the route of the railroad, but father was out near Ogden, Utah, and was present when they drove the golden spike, as the railroad's track laying was completed. He held a stake or something for General Grant at the ceremony."[19]

The Mormons, who had been making and selling whiskey since the 1850s, enjoyed their own spirits to celebrate the railroads joining. Josiah F. Gibbs was a Mormon and wrote in detail about his life during that time. He penned, "That the Saints comprising the city council had a hilarious time in celebrating the advent of the Union Pacific railroad in 1869, is proved by the following items under date of May 24th: To liquor on account of railroad celebration $81.00. To cigars on account of railroad celebration $25.00. To sundries on account of railroad celebration $235.00. An itemized account of the 'sundries' in the item of $235.00 would no doubt prove interesting."[20]

The transcontinental railroad was completed with a golden spike at Promontory Point, Utah Territory, on May 10, 1869. The two competing railroad companies—the Union Pacific and the Central Pacific—incented towns to grow along the line. The iron horse crossed the vast western territory, making travel more accessible and allowing improved quality in products for saloons, barware, ice, and ingredients. Towns provided goods and services for the railroad companies and later the passengers. NATIONAL ARCHIVES

The transcontinental railroad wasn't the only iron horse that traveled between Hell on Wheels towns with rough saloons and bad whiskey. The Kansas Hell on Wheels towns were reverse to those along the Union Pacific line. In this case these pioneers were determined to make a quick profit and move on to the next stop just after the tracks were laid and had no plans of settling down. When the new Atchison, Topeka & Santa Fe Railway was being built, it headed for Dodge City and with it came the transient ramble that made up the residents of a Hell on Wheels town. A newspaper report in 1873 noted there was a "peculiar" people located on the southwestern frontier of Kansas. They called them genuine roughs from all portions of the world. These men were considered cool, daring, lawless, and of a murderous disposition. They were feared by hopeful pioneers and businessmen who were attempting to set up and live in their small towns as the railroad billowed through. The paper reported, "The scenes of blood and murder that were once so common at Ellsworth and Sheridan when the Kansas Pacific Railway was being built are now being enacted upon the Atchison, Topeka, and Santa Fe Railway.... The class of people who follow immediately in the wake of the track builders, are a cosmopolitan class—a medley made up of roughs, rowdies, gamblers, speculators, saloon-keepers, and founders of towns, all sharp, gritty, and 'git and git' sort of people, who care for nothing except the almighty dollar."[21]

While many pioneers and emigrants were thrilled to have more railroads with more stops crisscrossing the country, not everyone was enamored with the amenities, or lack of amenities, at terminal stations. A *New York Tribune* reporter took the new transcontinental railroad bound for California and wrote a lengthy piece that appeared in the *Sacramento Daily Union*. The reporter wrote about his experience at one of the last Hell on Wheels terminals: "Promontory is neither city nor solitude, neither camp nor settlement. It is a bivouac without comfort, it is delay without rest. It is sun that scorches, and alkali dust that blinds. It is vile whisky, vile cigars, petty gambling and state newspapers at twenty-five cents apiece. It would drive a morbid mind to suicide. It is thirty tents upon the Great Sahara, sans trees, sans water, sans comfort, sans everything. In this horrible place were we detained in the afternoon. The neglect of the Central Pacific to make a close connection here will be shortly remedied, but it was inexcusable for a single week.... But we had the good fortune to find a sleeping car at Promontory, the second that ever passed over the line. At nearly every station through to Sacramento the people, attracted by its novelty, crowded to its doors and windows, eager to inspect it, and prompt to exclaim, 'Isn't it gay?' That beats the world!' We found it smooth running and comfortable, a vast improvement upon day coaches, but far inferior to Pullmans."[22]

By the 1870s George Pullman's luxury sleeper cars were being used on the Union Pacific line. Pullman cars not only afforded comfortable travel, but also opened up another avenue where whiskey and spirituous beverages could be procured and sold to passengers. Pullman cars included a baggage car, second-class coach, first-class coach, a ladies' car, sleepers, and a smoking car. The smoking cars were for the men who wanted to enjoy their cigars and pipes. They were also treated to a "refreshment buffet" to moisten the parched throats of the smokers. The smoking cars also served as a place where the male employees of the trains could take their lunches, sleep, or read during their downtime. A former conductor named Charles Walbourn wrote a book about his time as a Pullman conductor. He recalled, "Now we will say this train is composed of five cars, which makes also five porters to be relieved for rest, and there is only one man to relieve them and that is the conductor; or, first I will explain that a porter is supposed to sleep in the smoking-room and is to be off duty from 10:30 or 11 o'clock in the evening until 3 o'clock the next morning . . . and the conductor does guard in both of these cars and looks out for the wants of the passengers while the porters are asleep." He explained the reasoning for this: "I once worked at a place where we had to leave the building to get a decent drink of water. Now the wise employer of men is putting in reading and smoking rooms where the men can go and eat their lunch and read and rest instead of eating in the alley or going to saloons."[23]

Another conductor named Herbert Holderness recalled the smoking car all too well. He remembered that "the porter is dispatched to the buffet car with orders for wine, whisky, and bottled ale for seven people. Upon his return, after the pipes are recharged and lighted, with a fresh supply of cigars for those who smoke them, it is moved by the jolly man and seconded by his friend Bob

WINE LIST.

CHAMPAGNES

G. H. MUMM'S EXTRA DRY	PINTS,	$2.00
VEUVE CLICQUOT, Yellow Label	"	2.00
DELBECK & COMPANY'S "DELMONICO" ......Half	"	1.00

WHITE WINES
CRUSE AND FILS FRERES

HAUT SAUTERNES	"	1.00

CLARETS
CRUSE AND FILS FRERES

ST. JULIEN	"	.75
PONTET CANET	"	1.25

WHISKIES.

GROMMES & ULLRICH'S NATIONAL CLUB, Individual Bottle..	.20
GROMMES & ULLRICH'S WESTMORELAND RYE, Indiv'l Bottle	.20
HOUSE OF COMMONS, SCOTCH, Individual Bottle	.25
SAZERAC COCKTAILS-MANHATTAN, MARTINI, GIN, WHISKEY	.25

BUDWEISER (Anheuser-Busch) BEER	PINT,	.20
PABST'S MILWAUKEE EXPORT BEER	"	.20
BASS' PALE ALE, (White Label and Dog's Head)	"	.30
GUINNESS' DUBLIN STOUT	"	.30
BELFAST GINGER ALE	"	.25
JOHANNIS LITHIA WATER..	"	.25
HATHORN WATER	"	.25
APOLLINARIS WATER	"	.25
APOLLINARIS WATER, Splits	1-2 Pint	.15
APOLLINARIS LEMONADE, Splits..	"	.25
LEMONADE, Plain	Glass,	.15
EMERSON'S BROMO SELTZER		.15

IMPORTED CIGARS, 15c.   DOMESTIC CIGARS, 10c. and 2 for 25c.

RICHMOND STRAIGHT CUT CIGARETTES, 25c.

EGYPTIAN DEITIES No. 3, 25c.

IMPORTED NESTOR CIGARETTES, 40c.   SANITAS, 50c.

PLAYING CARDS, 50c.

Pullman cars offered elegant meals and an assortment of beverages. This
1901 list includes champagne, wine, whiskey, beer, and other refreshments. Note that whiskey is the only liquor offered. NEW YORK PUBLIC
LIBRARY DIGITAL COLLECTIONS

that everyone present tell a little story, and in obedience to the unanimous request of the assembled company, the jolly man relates for their benefit the story of 'A MIDNIGHT ROMANCE.' . . . Whereupon 'Billy,' the gentleman designated, shows his appreciation of some implied compliment by instantly producing two tall black bottles and a corkscrew, which is the signal for another yell and an onslaught on the whisky contained therein, and very soon, more bottles being forthcoming, the whole crowd is engaged in a drinking bout, during the progress of which the liveliest badinage, some of it not of the most refined character, is indulged in. In our capacity as conductor we are supposed to keep order, but it is of very little use trying to make ourselves heard, let alone understood. . . ." Some of the buffet items Pullmans offered by the turn of the century included National Club and Westmoreland whiskeys as well as Sazerac cocktails made with whiskey.[24]

Traveling on the railroads held a different experience for everyone and depended upon the class of service, like first-class or immigrant. The famous Irish playwright, novelist, poet, and whiskey imbiber Oscar Wilde penned, "Perhaps the most beautiful part of America is the West, to reach which, however, involves a journey by rail of six days, racing along tied to an ugly tin-kettle of a steam engine. I found but poor consolation for this journey in the fact that the boys who infest the cars and sell everything that one can eat— or should not eat—were selling editions of my poems vilely printed on a kind of grey blotting paper, for the low price of ten cents."[25]

America's new national highway was used by a variety of companies to ship their goods. The well-known catalog company Montgomery Ward even started selling whiskey and used to ship it from its warehouse in Chicago, Illinois, to points west. The spring/summer catalog of 1875 offered gin, bourbon whiskey, rye whiskey, brandy, and other spirits. Rye whiskey was sold by the gallon in six-gallon kegs. The cheapest was 90 percent rye whiskey at $1.75 per gallon and the most expensive was six-year-old rye at $5.50 per gallon.[26]

Elegant whiskeys from Kentucky and back East were served in the opulent Pullman dining cars. Circa 1894. LIBRARY OF CONGRESS

The bustling railroad town of Las Vegas, New Mexico, received supplies like the ones that Montgomery Ward shipped once the rails reached the town in 1879. Its history began when the first house was built by Miguel Romero in 1833. Soon, other Mexican emigrants living in San Miguel settled there. The town was called Nuestra Senora de las Dolores de Las Vegas. Las Vegas also sat along the Santa Fe Trail, and more pioneers decided to stop and settle; by 1870 there were about four thousand people calling Las Vegas home. On July 4, 1879, the first train of the Atchison, Topeka & Santa Fe chugged into town. A resident of the town, H. T. Wilson, wrote about the excitement:

On the 4th, the first train came in, and the "fate was sealed." The great train of freighters who were running between Las Vegas and Otero, Trinidad, West Las Animas and Kansas City were sent on their way to seek pastures more green in southern countries. The crack of the driver's whip, and rumbling of the bulky old stage, gave way to the shrill snort of the "iron horse," and whirl and whiz of the wonderful cars. The year 1879 will ever be remembered as the most eventful era in the history of the place. With the railroad came hordes of people, of every class and description. A new town sprang up near the depot, on the east side of the little river Rio Gallinas, on which Las Vegas is situated, and what was almost a wilderness, seemed in a day to be transformed to a metropolis with all the life, activity and industry of a new frontier town. Town lots were laid out in June, and building at once commenced; the sound of the hammer and saw as heard in all directions, and by the last of August, shanties of almost all sizes and descriptions were scattered all over the IQW tract of land about the depot, numbering near one hundred and fifty, with a population of nearly 1,000 new inhabitants. Many who were creeping into the stages of old decay, saw a railroad and train of cars for the first time. Dance houses, variety saloons, and every class of novel-

ties and amusements rushed in, carrying dread astonishment and often wondering consternation to the natives. Frightful broils, horrible orgies, fearful rows and murders became of common occurrence; freedom and gambling ran riot, and law had no sway. But improvements went on; money was plenty, but living was very high, from which many reaped a little fortune, while others lost what little they had on landing.[27]

Rock and Rye
with Billy the Kid

Sheriff Pat Garrett, the famous lawman who captured Billy the Kid, claimed that he and his posse drank Rock and Rye while they were chasing Billy.

"At last he [Francisco Arragon] invited my two companions to accompany him to his house, 'just across the street' where he promised to regale them with rock and rye, ad infinitum. Littler persuasion was produced, and after two or three libations, Don Francisco opened his combat with the windmills."

Source: *The Authentic Life of Billy the Kid.* Pat Floyd Garrett, 1882

By 1880 Las Vegas had grown to six thousand inhabitants. A host of colorful western characters visited Las Vegas, including John Henry "Doc" Holliday and William H. "Billy the Kid" Bonney. The advertisements for Las Vegas's saloons were many, and they offered all sorts of libations. Mr. R. G. McDonald noted that while he was back East he bought a large stock of fine whiskeys and was prepared to off them at a lower rate than anyone else in town. A comical endorsement from the *Las Vegas Gazette* was, "You Must Not Stay Away . . . from Bramm's because he has just received fresh cigars, imported and domestic;

all kinds of wines and whisky so old that it reminds you of the revolution when you drink it." That same paper warned about the dangers of consuming too much whiskey, writing, "The amount of whiskey that is swallowed daily in Las Vegas by all classes is enormous; including the better class of young men who were brought up back in the States to have a horror of the intoxicating cup. Buyers Beware! You can drink here without being noticed or being branded topers but the habit will get the better of you before you know it."[28]

The railroads capitalized on the fact that Las Vegans and Americans loved their liquor. Greater consumption meant that the railroads would have more goods to ship. *Scribner's* published a statistical atlas of the United States that detailed consumption and manufacture findings for 1880. It indicated that the total value of liquor produced in 1880 was $142,121,438, and while malted and fermented liquors, like wine and beer, made up most of that number, distilled liquors were $41,063,063 of the total produced. Compare that to the value given for coffee by the US government as of June 30, 1870, which was $24,234,879.[29] The states producing the most distilled spirits were Illinois, Kentucky, Indiana, and Ohio, and all shipped their products west. In that same report it was noted that revenue earned from those products varied from state to state. Not surprising Illinois earned the most revenue at $6.6 per capita. Ohio ranked second at $4.56, Kentucky came in third at $4.28, and Indiana at $2.9 per capita (person).

In this 1880 report, the consumption of distilled and fermented spirits was tracked from 1864 to 1880. It's interesting to note that distilled spirits consumption in 1864 was at an all-time high when 2.5 gallons was being consumed per capita. It fell to less than half a gallon per person until 1869 when it jumped back up to about 1.5 gallons per person. The following year it rose to just over 2 gallons, but from 1870 to 1880 Americans were consuming between 1 and 1.5 gallons of distilled spirits. Beer and wine were consumed at a rate of about 3 gallons per person in 1864, and with a steady increase, rose to almost 8 gallons per person in 1880. Using the previously mentioned coffee values, that equated to 15 gallons of coffee on average per person.[30]

Railroads also capitalized on the fact that grain was a much-needed commodity to make whiskey. According to Mark Wymond in his book, *Railroad Valuation and Rates*:

> *The territory comprised within the grain-growing areas in the north central states and at least as far west as the Missouri River, had been very generally settled up by the early '70s. The production of grain at this time vastly exceeded the needs of these communities, but the cost of transporting the surplus to the eastern states and the Atlantic ports for export was prohibitive at the rates then current, on account of the long haul involved. The railroad business serving the grangers, who were the first major farm organization, as the territory was unprofitable and in a bad way financially at this time. It was during this period that the price of corn was so low in some of the states within this area that it was used as fuel. The railroads were incentivized to make profits by the grain surpluses out West and established "granger" roads that were extensions of the existing railroads. Providing a market for this surplus made it profitable to extend the area of agricultural operation in producing more grain, involving the construction of extensions of the existing railroads.[31]*

As an example, 3,623,055 bushels of rye and 17,649,269 bushels of corn were used to make distilled spirits in 1880. Between the states of Arizona, California, Colorado, Missouri, Nebraska, Oklahoma, Oregon, and Texas, 248,285 bushels of corn were used to create distilled liquors in the 1890s. Those same states used 31,171 bushels of rye to make distilled spirits. Missouri produced the most spirits using corn, while California used the most rye to create their liquor. The railroads made all this possible.

This cartoon was symbolic of the impact railroads had on the western whiskey market. Circa 1880s. LIBRARY OF CONGRESS

For some railroad towns, whiskey was more than an occasional nuisance or a moral smirch—it was a very dangerous drug. In places like Soda Springs, Idaho, the arrival of a railroad brought a flood of humanity in all varieties. Many of the proper citizens saw their civic dreams ruined by sleazy saloons and lowlifes "just traveling through." Soda Springs was transformed by the railroad reaching it, much to the dismay of many. In 1881 it was a quiet little hamlet where scarcely a noise louder than the bubbling of the health-giving springs could be heard. However, once the Utah & Northern Railroad reached it around August 1882, all that changed. Basic food prices and provisions rose nearly 100 percent in value. The only cheap thing was whiskey. A resident at the time wrote, "I look from my window upon half a dozen saloons. At night, I sleep with a pistol under my pillow and a double barrel shotgun by my side, kept awake by the shrieks and howls of drunken men. These wretched bummers, who have come here to build up the town have torn down or defaced the spring houses, defiled the waters, and for the present, at least, made the place almost uninhabitable. Shooting in the saloons is of such common occurrence that it is little noticed, but horse stealing is a crime that seldom goes without speedy punishment if the thieves can be caught."

In addition to whiskey and wood, coal was becoming an important commodity for the railroads, so it's not surprising that railroad companies began buying up lots near coal deposits. In 1887 Frank Mondell discovered coal near Cambria (located north of Newcastle), Wyoming. His discovery gained the attention of the Lincoln Land Company, which was a subsidiary of the Chicago, Burlington and Quincy Railroad. In 1889 they built a seven-mile spur from Newcastle north to Cambria. The town of Newcastle, or "Tubtown," was known as a "tough place to live." Two men, Will Whealan and Joe Reubens, had recently returned from a trip to that locale and gave an account to a newspaper. They said the land and location were beautiful and were convinced that the city would one day be a thriving and bustling community. However, it wasn't there yet, and they noted that "pandemonium reigns from sunset to sunrise." No more than 150 people called it home, and they were the toughest of the tough. A license fee of $150 per month was required to run a faro game, but no one could afford the stakes to play. Instead, the locals spent their money playing poker and "swilling" beer and whiskey. Several dance houses flourished, and drunken binges that included shooting out the lights were common. It was noted, "Nobody has been killed yet, but as pay day takes place this week, every confidence is entertained that the coroner will have two or three jobs before the week is out."[32]

Despite being seen negatively by some pioneers, the railroads helped fuel the progress in making whiskey a full-fledged commodity. The two were interwoven—each needing the other to keep progressing. Whiskey distillers could ship their product to a large volume of pioneers as the railroads increased their lines and tracks. At the same time, the railroad needed revenue from businesses like the grangers, distillers, coopers, and bottle makers to keep expanding. By the 1890s whiskey was being shipped all over America. Eastern distillers were sending their products to big cities in the West and western distributors were shipping to locales across the frontier and to foreign countries. In just the month of April 1892, according to the *Pacific Wine and Spirit Review,* the Southern Pacific Railroad delivered 578 barrels of whiskey to San Francisco consignees. The firm of C.W. Craig & Company received the largest shipment with 191 barrels. Nationally, whiskey exports for the month of February were just under 150,000 proof gallons, which was valued at about $117,000. In May, the *Review* felt distribution prospects were better and reported, "Distribution is going on at a fairly rapid rate despite the fact that this is the season when slackening in the trade is expected. The recent visit of so many distillers and distillers' agents from Kentucky has had a quickening effect on the trade in straight bourbons, and the results of these trips will no doubt be felt still more in the fall. Business may be called in a fairly good condition, and prospects never better. We have assured large crops throughout the interior of California, in Oregon, Washington and other states and territories of the Coast. Money is easy, and after the harvests are well in hand, the best Fall trade ever known should follow. This will be still further stimulated by the promised railroad development."[33]

By the middle of 1892, the *Pacific Wine and Spirit Review* reported that while the first six months of 1892 were better than the previous year, whiskey showed the most growth. They noted that imports by sea had fallen off, but that imports by rail were on the rise and more than compensated for the decrease by sea. By the end of June railroads had transported 950 cases, 10,310 full barrels, and 1,138 half barrels. The *Review* stated, "This shows how rapidly the direct business by rail is growing."[34]

While the railroads and whiskey jointly expanded the West and turned whiskey into an important commodity, it fell out of favor as temperance, prohibitions, increased regulation, and market consolidation rolled west. The twentieth century ushered in a new era when it came to whiskey. State prohibition laws and eventually national Prohibition were passed and brought another chapter of scrutiny, economics, and opportunities to control markets. When the repeal of Prohibition allowed whiskey back on the market, it was regulated and mass produced, and the love affair between the American West and whiskey was all but over. It can be said, though, that this golden elixir threaded western towns like the railroads threaded the country together.

CHAPTER SEVEN

Fast Forward:
Whiskey in the Modern West

WHISKEY HAS BEEN A PART OF AMERICAN HISTORY SINCE THE
nation's infancy. Its story began with early colonists who found
ways to distill spirits from their agricultural bounty, continued
with George Washington and the Whiskey Rebellion, and traveled west as trailblazers and pioneers explored the vast expanse
west of the Mississippi River. It influenced the commodity
market, the cattle industry, and the railroads, and it fueled the
temperance and prohibition movements. The history of America
cannot be told with mentioning American whiskey and how it
influenced our nation.

Despite the turbulence of the past centuries and the ups and
downs of the industry's cycle, whiskey consistently manages to
find a role in America's story. Whiskey had a formative effect on
the character of the American West, where it became a fixture of
the western saloon and symbolic of the rough and wild terrain.

When the Anti-Saloon League, temperance movements, and
Prohibition era shifted the industry from large-scale regulated
growth to illicit markets and illegal production, society resisted
being forced to give up their spirituous libations, and makers and
drinkers simply went underground. They socialized and imbibed
in Speakeasys, "soda parlors," and behind closed doors in private

homes. Prohibition had just about dried up the straight whiskey supply in the United States, allowing other spirits products to take its place. Those that seized the opportunity were products much cheaper and easier to make, such as gin and Canadian whiskies like Canadian Club, became mainstays in the market. The blended multi-grain liquors typically contained a small percentage of rye with a larger portion of more neutral spirits.[1]

After the Second World War, the end of Prohibition and the rise of scientific innovation and industrial efficiency led to a sustained period of quantity-driven whiskey production. Only a few exceptional products emerged, such as Bill Samuels Sr.'s small-batch Maker's Mark, in its wax-sealed bottles. In the mid-80s, Buffalo Trace Distillery released the nation's first super-premium, single-barrel straight bourbon since Prohibition. Called Blanton's it wasn't an immediate hit, but it was newsworthy and it opened the mind-set of mainstream customers. A decade later a handful of other super-premium products had emerged, such as Basil Hayden, Bakers, Bookers, Woodford Reserve, and Knob Creek. A handful of dedicated distillers who were passionate about the quality of their product stayed true to the art of making good whiskey and have become modern-day celebrities. Some still attend the whiskey shows, lead seminars, and are working on new product releases. Jim Rutledge, formerly with Four Roses, Booker Noe at Jim Beam, Elmer T. Lee of Ancient Age, and Lincoln Henderson at Early Times are just a few of the present-day rock stars in the industry. It is also interesting to note Woodford Reserve was created on the same historic site where Crow and Pepper's origins were rooted, owned by Brown-Forman, who restored the distillery including the addition of traditional copper pot stills, much like the originals.

Today a modern era of quality super-premium products has emerged, growing in tandem with the gourmet food culture and desire for authentic goods. The whiskey industry is experiencing a renaissance of distillers and their spirits—and a significant number of distillers are now located in the American West. Single-barrel bourbons, single-malt Scotches, whiskey festivals with educational whiskey seminars, whiskey magazines, and much improved and expanded distillery tours are paving the way for the small-batch distiller and the American brown spirit's revival. In January 2017, there were 1,037 distillery permits west of the Mississippi, nearly 50 percent of the total nationwide. The two top states were California, with 291, followed by New York with 156 and with Kentucky listing only 65 (Colorado, Oregon, Texas, and Washington each have more than Kentucky). In 1895, the Bureau of Statistics reported that 90 percent of distilled spirits were produced east of the Mississippi River, notably in Kentucky and Illinois.[2]

Small-batch distillers are being propelled by a combination of modern trends in consumer products, including celebrating local heritage and interest in unique artisanal products. The "foodie movement" and emphasis on buying local, quality products from people who share details about their origins also plays a role. Novel product innovations have also allowed the smaller distilleries to gain recognition. Modern consumers value being educated about what they are purchasing; they enjoy buying local, respect quality and premium businesses, and desire unique experiences. This cycle also follows the drive for consumers to push for authenticity and trending away from mass-produced impersonal items.

Whiskey distillers appear to be more ambitious today than they were a century ago. The most popular types of whiskey on the market are bourbon, rye, and malt whiskey (Scotch in Scotland), but increasingly, distillers are being innovative and creating experimental varieties. Some of today's artisan distillers are experimenting with blue corn, oats, quinoa, amaranth, and other exotic ingredients. Balcones Distilling in Waco, Texas, created their Baby Blue whiskey from roasted heirloom blue corn, and their Brimstone whiskey is smoked with sunbaked Texas scrub oak. While some distillers are using exotic ingredients that the pioneers didn't even know existed, others are using technological distilling methods. It's quite possible that western frontier whiskey makers experimented with the maturation process by adding smoked wood chips or tree bark to the barrel to speed the flavor process, as is being done today at Boothill Distillery in Dodge City, Kansas. They use 75 percent corn, 25 percent wheat whiskey mash, and let it age in thirty-gallon barrels for a month with added oak spirals for extra infusion. While accelerating the maturation phase of whiskey is not a new pursuit, the innovative and unorthodox manner in which this is performed is gaining attention in the new frontier. Whiskey makers likely never imagined using sonic maturation, the idea of agitating the barrels with loud speakers and intense music, now being practiced at Tuthilltown Spirits Distillery in Gardiner, New York. The aging process postpones the business's income stream, which entices distillers to seek more cost-effective ways to reduce maturation time. Some distillers rock their barrels on a boat at sea, in an environment of high heat, allowing them to be agitated by Mother Nature, such as the recently released Jefferson's Ocean product line. Another current method being used by Cleveland Whiskey of Cleveland, Ohio, employs a pressure cooker to pressure-age whiskey in attempts to speed up the maturation cycle. Many others used reduced barrel sizes, which increases the wood-to-liquid surface area ratio.

Today, a number of American whiskies from all over the country—many with western roots—are being presented at world whiskey festivals and are being featured on high-end bar shelves. Distillers of the twenty-first century are pioneering entrepreneurs with a passion and dedication to excellence in quality and brand development. An early trailblazer, High West Distillery in Park City, Utah, helped to open the western frontier with unique premium products that embrace the spirit of the West and a state-of-the-art visitor's center that focuses on educating consumers by helping them to appreciate whiskey with good food. Whiskey flights and high-end whiskey paired menus are offered. Other historic western distilleries are being resurrected, like the Holladay Distillery in Weston, Missouri. They've been in business since 1856 and today are distilling Ben Holladay's original recipe to create their Holladay 1856 bourbon. The same is true of the J. Rieger distillery, which has resurrected their 1887 location in Kansas City, Missouri. They are a modern-day rectifier.

In addition to embracing the "small batch is better" theory, distilleries have been giving a nod to some of the men who pioneered whiskey making in the United States. Products such as the Colonel E. H. Taylor was rereleased by Buffalo Trace to recognize Taylor as a founding father of the bourbon industry for his innovative marketing. Heaven Hill's Elijah Craig single barrel promotes full-flavored small-batch bourbon to honor the Baptist preacher. Craig founded his distillery in 1789 and was credited with the "true Kentucky Bourbon" process of aging whiskey in charred oak barrels for extended periods of time. While historians cannot prove this story, it and many others like it are common. Legends often make good stories, which in turn attract the twenty-first-century whiskey drinker who is looking for a connection to the past. Evan Williams's whiskey celebrates the first recorded commercial distillery in Louisville, Kentucky, built in 1783.[3]

Educated consumers want to know as much about the product as possible, so distillers are trending toward open and authentic communication, labels with specific information, and straightforward educational tours and websites. This is quite different from the whiskey industry of the nineteenth century where falsely marketed, adulterated, and doctored-up products were the norm. Discerning drinkers are interested in information about all aspects of where the whiskey derives its flavor, and distillers are providing detailed information, many even presented on their labels. Details such as type of wood used in barrel finish, char level, batch and bottle number, elevation or position in the warehouse, exact mash bill recipe, source and age of straight whiskies in the blend, and even tasting notes have been included in the labels. Once again, science and chemistry are being employed to improve efficiency and flavor. Buffalo Trace's master distiller made the comment, "The thought is to identify every variable, which we may never do," says Harlen Wheatley, Buffalo Trace's master distiller. "But we're on the trail," and he says the company's chemists have found about 300 different compounds, and have identified some 200 of them." Another perspective puts emphasis on the time-honored process of natural oxidation and barrel aging. As the increased wood-to-liquor ratio speeds the infusion of the wood flavors, that's only part of the aging process. The other part occurs during oxidation, when air gets in through the barrel's semi-porous wood and interacts with the spirit. Corn (bourbon is by law at least 51 percent corn) has long, complex, oily molecules, which give young bourbon its round and vegetal funk. During a chemical reaction called esterification, these chains break down and reconfigure, then react anew with the wood, adding depth and additional flavors. The much-debated thought is that this oxidation process can't be rushed with smaller barrels.[4]

The past decade has seen a resurrection of small-batch artisanal whiskeys that celebrate whiskey's American heritage and offer unique and bold tastes. An evolution that has come full circle from frontier times when small distillers, rectifiers, and blenders outnumbered the giants. Industrial efficiency, combined with political and economic factors (including Prohibition), shifted emphasis away from small and craft to large production facilities with lower costs and more consistent flavor profiles as the twentieth century dawned. The modern trend on the frontier is not to return to quantity and lower cost, but to emphasize quality and innovation.

CHAPTER EIGHT

Belly Up to the Bar:
Cocktails of the West

THE SURGE IN POPULARITY OF DISTILLED SPIRITS HAS CREATED a revival of the cocktail culture and veneration for the modern mixologist. There is also a resurgence of vintage cocktails, glassware, bartending books, and speakeasies—and the Old West shouldn't be left out of the image. While Hollywood usually doesn't depict a cowboy walking up to the bar in a western saloon to order a cocktail, the reality was that they were quite common, especially after the very popular bartender's guide *How to Mix Drinks or the Bon-Vivant's Companion* was published in 1862 by "Professor" Jerry Thomas. Jerry was a skilled bartender and showman who started his career with saloons in New York and then made his way west to San Francisco with many other hopefuls during the gold rush. Thomas's bartender's guidebook was so popular that it was updated with later editions and has recently been revived in the whiskey cocktail trend.

There were over two hundred recipes that were recorded as "styles" rather than under the category of cocktails, which had a category of their own. The Punch, Sour, Flip, Shrub, Julep, Toddy, Daisy, and other cocktail drinks were listed in more of an instruction manual for the saloonkeeper rather than a trade book marketed at large. Like boutique whiskeys, Thomas's book is now quite popular among home bar aficionados.

At least four well-known cocktails originated in the West before Prohibition and are still popular today. The martini is one, but it does not include whiskey and purportedly has its roots near San Francisco Bay, originating during the gold rush era in Martinez, California. Another famous non-whiskey cocktail with origins in San Francisco dates back to the 1830s. The Pisco Punch was made from a type of brandy called Pisco, which is a Peruvian brandy from the winemaking regions of Peru or Chile.

San Francisco attracted a variety of pioneers to its bustling city, and they came with the desire to make a name for themselves. Pioneers tried to find ways to stand out from the crowd, and mixologists of the day did that by creating their own cocktails. Another cocktail pioneer from San Francisco was made famous by publishing a book on bartending and for his invented drink called the Boothby. William T. "Cocktail" Boothby, author of *Cocktail Boothby's American Bartender: The New Anchor Distilling Edition* of 1891, was head bartender of the grand Palace Hotel as well as other posh saloons around town. He was arguably one of the city's premier pre-Prohibition mixologists. The Boothby cocktail is made from vermouth, bourbon, and bitters and topped with a floater of champagne that's garnished with an orange twist. When his book came out in 1891, an ad appeared in the *San Francisco Call* that stated, "Bar-keepers—you're not in it if you don't read 'Cocktail Boothby's American Bartender.' 50 cents; at all newsstands."

Another popular throwback bartender book is from a somewhat rival to Jerry Thomas named Harry Johnson. Johnson went west during the gold rush to seek his fortune, but after unsuccessful attempts in other occupations, opened his own establishment by the late 1860s in Chicago. After a tragic fire burned down his saloon, he moved back East, where he opened the Little Jumbo on the Bowery in New York. In 1882 he published the *Bartender's Manual on How to Mix Drinks* and updated this in 1888 as

This is the Boothby Cocktail along with a copy of his original *American Bartender* book. PHOTO COURTESY OF PALACE HOTEL, SAN FRANCISCO

the *New and Improved Illustrated Bartender's Manual.* His book included many recipes but also offered recommendations and advice to bartenders for dealing with customers, dress and etiquette, and equipment; he even published a bilingual version in German for a large segment of the bartending population.

Modern whiskey cocktail trends have revitalized craft-made drinks like shrubs and bitters, slings, punches, and many more vintage drinks originally published in the late 1800s. Once again, the modern mixologist has a respected position in a popular trade where knowledge combined with showmanship is revered. The return of American whiskeys to top shelves and featured cocktail lists has solidified their prominent position. The modern distiller is adored much like the heroes of the nostalgic West who played a significant role in bringing whiskey to the frontier. Whiskey, whether in the past or present, is making American history. It is once again among the most popular distilled spirit in America— just like it once was in the American West.

Whiskey Punch
Serves 2

While at Fort Bridger on the Oregon Trail, trapper James Beckwourth served the Cheyenne chief Mo-he-nes-to (The Elk That Calls) and his wife "whisky punch, well-flavored with spices."

Juice of 1 lemon
4 ounces whiskey
2 teaspoons sugar
2 dashes brandy

Shake all ingredients together. Strain into glasses or goblets that have been filled with shaved or crushed ice. Garnish with fruit.

Source: Adapted from *Harry Johnson's Bartender's Manual*, 1882

Blue Blazer
Makes 1 drink

Professor Jerry Thomas, as he was affectionately referred to, demonstrated creative and artistic cocktail inventions such as his famous *Blue Blazer*, which is whiskey mixed with sugar water, lit on fire, and tossed between silver mugs to create a dazzling stream of blue flames. He also crafted his own bitters and infusions for his drinks.

Use two large silver-plated mugs with handles.
1 wine-glass (5 ounces) of Scotch whiskey
1 wine-glass (5 ounces) boiling water

Put the whiskey and the boiling water in one mug, ignite the liquid with fire, and while blazing mix both ingredients by pouring them four or five times from one mug to the other, as represented in the cut. If well done this will have the appearance of a continued stream of liquid fire.

Sweeten with one teaspoonful of pulverized white sugar and serve in a small tumbler, with a piece of lemon peel.

Source: Adapted from *The Bar-Tenders' Guide: A Complete Cyclopaedia of Plain and Fancy Drinks*, Jerry Thomas, 1862.

JERRY THOMAS' OWN DECANTER BITTERS
Makes 3½ cups
These bitters appear to be served as a stand-alone drink as well as being used for other cocktails.

3 cups rum
1 pound of raisins
2 ounces of cinnamon
1 ounce Sampson's snake-root or substitute birch bark, quassia wood, or wild cherry bark
1 lemon and 1 orange, cut in slices
1 ounce of cloves
1 ounce allspice
750 ml Santa Cruz rum

Fill decanter with rum and add the remaining ingredients. Bottle and serve out in pony glasses. As fast as the bitters is used, fill up again with rum.

Source: Adapted from *The Bar-Tender's Guide: A Complete Cyclopaedia of Plain and Fancy Drinks*, Jerry Thomas, 1862.

BOOTHBY COCKTAIL
Makes 1 drink
This cocktail was created by mixologist William "Cocktail" Boothby while he tended bar at the elegant Palace Hotel in San Francisco.

1¼ ounces whiskey
1 ounce Italian vermouth
2 drops angostura bitters
2 dashes orange bitters
Ice
1 ounce champagne or sparkling wine, chilled
1 stemmed maraschino cherry

Place the whiskey, vermouth and bitters in a mixing glass. Fill two-thirds with ice, stir, and strain into a chilled cocktail glass. Add the cherry and then float the champagne on top.

Source: *The American Bar-Tender*, William "Cocktail Boothby," 1891, courtesy of the Palace Hotel, San Francisco, California.

ORANGE CORDIAL
Makes about 10 gallons
As a compound a cordial is nothing more than a spirit impregnated with the essential oil of the ingredients.

Take 5 gallons pure proof rectified whiskey, add ½ pound fresh lemon-peel, 2 pounds dried orange-peel, and 3 pounds fresh orange-peel. Let stand for 10 or 14 days, then drain. Add 3 gallons soft water, 1½ gallons syrup, and let stand for another 10 to 14 days.

Source: Adapted from *Six Hundred Receipts: Worth Their Weight in Gold*, 1867

Rock and Rye Cocktail
Makes as many as you like
This drink must be very carefully prepared, and care must be taken to procure the best rock candy syrup, and also the best of rye whiskey, as this drink is an effectual remedy for sore throats, etc.

½ tablespoon rock candy syrup
Rye whiskey

Place syrup in a whiskey glass and place a spoon in it. Pour as much of the whiskey as you like over the syrup. Or as Johnson says, "Hand the bottle of Rye whiskey to the customer, to help himself."

Source: *Harry Johnson's New and Improved Illustrated Bartender's Manual*, 1888

Whiskey Toddy
Serves 1
This cocktail was one of the most popular during the 19th century.

½ teaspoon sugar
1 teaspoon water
1–2 ice cubes
1 wine glass of whiskey (6 ounces)

Place sugar in a whiskey glass and add the water. Stir to dissolve and then add the ice. Pour the whiskey into the glass and stir. *Note:* The original recipe instructions read, "The most proper way for the bartender is to dissolve the sugar into the water only, and leave a spoon in the glass, hand out the bottle of whiskey to the customer to help himself."

Source: Adapted from *Harry Johnson's New and Improved Illustrated Bartender's Manual*, 1882

Whiskey Hot
Makes 1 drink

This hot whiskey drink could warm a pioneer from his nose to his toes.

1 to 2 lumps sugar with a little hot water to dissolve the sugar well
⅔ cup hot water
2 ounces whiskey
1 lemon peel strip
Nutmeg
(Use a hot whiskey glass.)

Dissolve the sugar in the water and fill the glass and mix well. Squeeze and throw in the lemon peel and grate a little nutmeg on top.

Whiskey Sour
Makes 1 drink

The whiskey sour was popular on the frontier and has been a favorite ever since.

Juice of ½ lemon
½ teaspoon powdered sugar
2 ounces whiskey
Carbonated water
Berries

Dissolve the sugar with a little of the carbonated water. Combine all ingredients and shake with crushed ice. Strain into a 6-ounce glass. Fill with carbonated water and top with berries.

Source: Both recipes adapted from *Harry Johnson's New and Improved Illustrated Bartenders' Manual*, 1888

MONONGAHELA WHISKEY

Take 36 gallons pure spirits, and add ¼ pound young hyson tea, 6 pounds dried peaches, baked brown, not burned, 4 pounds loaf sugar, 4 ounces cloves, 4 ounces cinnamon. Mix them all together, and stir them well for 3 or 4 days, and in a few weeks it will be good.

You can put double or triple the quantity of flavouring in, and then take 3, 4, 5, or 6 gallons of it and pour it into a barrel of pure rectified whiskey, and add 2 pounds loaf sugar to each barrel. The longer your flavouring will lie, the better.

APPLE WHISKEY

Take 30 gallons pure rectified whiskey, from 5 to 10 degrees above proof; add 4½ gallons pure apple whiskey, 1½ pints simple syrup, 2 good pineapples (the juice of them only). Mix thoroughly, and let stand for 2 weeks. Then ready for use.

CHERRY BRANDY

Take 10 gallons pure rectified whiskey, 13 quarts wild cherries, bruised; let stand 8 days; strain it, and add 6 pounds loaf sugar, and 2 gallons water.

FRENCH BRANDY

Take 10 gallons pure spirits, ½ pint tincture of bitter almonds, 2½ gallons good brandy; mix, and colour with sugar-colouring.

Source: Recipes from *Six Hundred Receipts: Worth Their Weight in Gold*, 1867

Temperance Punch
Makes 1 gallon

Temperance drinks became very popular for those who wanted to drink "cocktails."

6 cups boiling water
2 tablespoons green tea
6 lemons, peeled and pared
2 oranges, peeled and pared
2 cups sugar
2 cups cherry juice
Seltzer water

Pour the water over the tea and let sit for 5 minutes. Remove tea. Add the lemons, oranges, sugar, and juice and stir until sugar dissolves. Fill glasses ¾ of the way and top with seltzer.

Source: *Idaho Daily Statesman*, May 22, 1900

Pink Tea
Makes 1½ gallons

This recipe was listed with temperance drinks, but rum and whiskey make it anything but.

2 cups rock candy
4 lemons, juiced and peeled
1 orange, sliced
6 ounces whiskey
6 ounces rum
4 cups freshly boiled green tea
2 cups claret wine
2 cups carbonated mineral water
Strawberries and candied cherries

Combine candy, lemons, orange, whiskey, rum, and tea into a glass container and chill for 12 hours. Strain and add the claret and water. Fill the glasses and drop in a strawberry and two candied cherries.

Source: *Idaho Daily Statesman*, May 22, 1900

CROSS COUNTRY
Makes 2 gallons
This punch with its mix of fruits and vegetables was refreshing during the summer months.

Peel of 1 medium cucumber
1 pineapple, peeled and chopped
Juice and pulp of 4 oranges
Juice of 12 limes, strained
Peel of 1 lemon
4 cups rock candy
2 cups whiskey
2 cups rum or gin
6 cups boiling water
2 cups seltzer or mineral water

Place cucumber peel, pineapple, oranges, lime juice, lemon peel, rock candy, whiskey, and rum to a non-metal container that will not crack. Let sit for 6 hours. Strain and pour the boiling water over it. Chill for 3 hours and then put into a serving bowl with a large chunk of ice and add seltzer.

Source: *Idaho Daily Statesman*, May 22, 1900

Golden Elixir of the West
Makes 1 drink

Evidence and trends show that whiskey is once again at the front of the bar scene and in cocktail making. Sherry Monahan has created a signature whiskey cocktail for you to enjoy as you celebrate the history of whiskey in the West!

2 ounces whiskey
1 ounce triple sec
1 tablespoon agave syrup
1 tablespoon fresh-squeezed lime juice
¼ cup fresh-squeezed orange juice, strained

Combine all ingredients in a shaker and shake for 1 to 2 minutes. Serve in a highball glass over ice and garnish with a fresh orange peel.

APPENDIX

Liquor Laws and the Old West

NORTH DAKOTA LIQUOR LAWS, 1895
From the *Annual Report of the Commissioner of Labor*, 1898

The manufacture and importation of intoxicating liquors for sale or gift, and the keeping, selling, or offering of same for sale, etc., prohibited. City councils have the power to forbid and punish the soiling or disposing of liquors to any liquor, servant, insane, idiotic, or distracted person, habitual drunkard or intoxicated person; to provide for fines not exceeding $100 in any one case for violation of ordinances, etc.

Misdemeanor to expose liquors to sale or gift within one mile of the place where any religious assembly shall be actually convened for religious worship; does not apply to a duly licensed place in which accused shall have actually resided on the business.

Fines from $50 to $100 for selling or disposing of liquors on day of any general, special, or local election. Those bringing of liquors into the penitentiary or giving same to any inmate, except on written direction or order of the physician, is forbidden.

Misdemeanor to sell liquors within, or to bring same into, with intent to sell them therein, any courthouse while session of court is being held therein, any jail or prison, or any building used at the time for holding an election or canvassing the votes.

Misdemeanor to adulterate or dilute liquor with fraudulent intent to offer, or to cause or permit it to be offered for sale as unadulterated or undiluted, and to fraudulently sell or keep or offer the same for sale as unadulterated or undiluted.

It is unlawful for anyone to sell or barter liquors for medicinal, scientific, or mechanical purposes, without obtaining a druggist's permit therefor from the county judge, who can only grant such permits to registered pharmacists lawfully and in good faith engaged in the business of a druggist. Physicians may give prescriptions for liquors or may administer same in cases of actual need. Prescription must state nature of disease for which liquor is given. Fine of not less than $300 nor more than $800 on any physician violating above provisions. Druggists holding permits can sell only upon written or printed affidavit of applicant, and must make but one sale and one delivery upon any one affidavit. He must permit no drinking on his premises or in any place under his control. He may sell liquors in quantities not less than one gallon to any other druggist in the State holding a permit. Applicants' affidavits are to be made before the druggist or assistant making the sale on printed blanks to be furnished to the druggist by the county auditor at actual cost of the same. They shall be in series of 100 each, numbered from 1 to 100 consecutively, and bound in book form.

Montana Liquor Laws, 1895
From the *Annual Report of the Commissioner of Labor*, 1898

No license required of physicians or druggists for liquor used or sold for medicinal purposes.

Fines between $50 and $500 for selling liquors during any part of a day set apart for any general, special, or municipal election during the hours when the polls are open.

Misdemeanor to sell or furnish liquors in a theater or other place of amusement, or to employ, procure, or cause to be employed a female to sell or furnish liquors in such place.

Fines between $5 and $500 for selling or disposing of liquors within one mile of any camp or field meeting for religious worship during the time of such meeting. Does not apply to sales at a regular place of business established prior to the meeting referred to.

Misdemeanor to adulterate or dilute liquors with the fraudulent intent to offer or cause the same to be offered for sale as unadulterated and undiluted, or to sell, keep, or offer same for sale as unadulterated or undiluted.

Fines up to $100 for selling or disposing of liquors within two miles of any railroad in the course of construction or on which tracks are being laid; does not apply within the limits of any city or town.

Misdemeanor to commence or carry on any business for which a license is required without first securing such license.

Kansas Liquor Laws, 1889
From the *Annual Report of the Commissioner of Labor*, 1898

Manufacture and sale of intoxicating liquors, except for medicinal, scientific, and mechanical purposes, forever prohibited.

Mayor and councils of cities of the first class have power to prohibit and suppress tippling shops, saloons, dram shops, and clubrooms.

Up to $100 fine for selling or disposing of liquors within one mile of a camp or field meeting for religious worship. Does not apply to tavern keepers exercising their calling nor to distillers or manufacturers prosecuting their regular trade at their places of business.

Illegal to keep open any ale or porter house, grocery, or tippling shop, or to sell or retail liquors on Sunday.

Illegal to fraudulently adulterate wine or liquors, for the purpose of sale, with any substance injurious to health.

Illegal to sell or dispose of liquors within the unorganized counties or territories of the State. Between $50 and $200 of said fine to be paid to informer.

Unlawful to sell liquors for medicinal, etc., purposes except in case of druggists who have obtained a permit from probate judge so to do.

Physician may give prescription for liquor or may administer it himself. Illegal for a physician to give prescription or administer liquor except in case of actual need, or for the purpose of enabling any person to evade any provision of law.

Druggists holding permit can only sell upon affidavit of applicant setting forth purpose for which the liquor is required, etc. But one sale to be made on one affidavit. Must not allow liquor to be drunk on premises.

All places where liquors are manufactured, sold, or disposed of in violation of law, and where people are permitted to resort for the purpose of drinking liquor as a beverage, are declared to be common nuisances, and shall be shut up and abated as such.

Illegal to keep or assist in keeping by himself or in association with others, a clubroom, etc., where liquor is received or kept for the use, sale, etc., by, or for division in any manner among its members, and for using, selling, or disposing of liquor so received and kept, or assisting in selling or disposing of such liquor.

Illegal to receive any order for liquors from, or contract for the sale of liquors to, any person not authorized to sell same; druggists selling to any person after receiving notice from the guardian or any relative of such person that he uses liquor as a beverage, said notice forbidding sale to be made to him; treating, or giving liquor to, a minor except by father, mother, guardian, or a physician for medical purposes; the carrying or delivering liquors to any person to be sold in violation of this act by any employee of a common carrier.

Illegal to sell or dispose of liquors to an Indian, unless directed by a physician for medical purposes. Does not apply in case of Indians who are citizens of the United States or of the State of Kansas.

Illegal to sell or deliver liquors to a prisoner by a sheriff, jailer, or keeper of a prison, unless on written certificate of a physician.

UTAH LIQUOR LAWS, 1888
From the *Annual Report of the Commissioner of Labor*, 1898

The city council of any incorporated city has the power (1) to license, regulate, and tax the manufacturing, selling, or disposing of liquors, to determine the amount to be paid for an annual license, said license not to extend beyond the municipal year in which it is granted, and when such city license is granted no county license shall be required to enable person so licensed to sell within limits of the city; (2) to punish and prohibit the selling or disposing of liquors to any minor, insane or idiotic person, habitual drunkard, or person intoxicated; (3) to regulate the inspection of liquors, and (4) to pass all necessary ordinances, rules, and regulations to carry into effect all powers conferred by this section and to enforce obedience to same by fines which shall not exceed $300 for each offense.

Later laws included fines for anyone selling liquor in the auditorium or lobbies of any theater, museum, circus, etc. It was illegal to employ, procure, or cause to be employed or procured, any person to so sell liquors, erecting or keeping a booth, tent, stall, or other contrivance. Sales within one mile of a religious gathering place or operating a saloon or liquor business on Sunday was prohibited. Procuring, or employing any female to play for hire, drink, or gain, upon any musical instrument, or to dance, promenade, or otherwise exhibit herself in any drinking saloon was illegal. It was a misdemeanor to adulterate or dilute liquors or any article useful in compounding them with a fraudulent intent to offer the same, or to cause or permit the same to be offered, for sale as unadulterated or undiluted, and to sell, keep or offer such liquor for sale as unadulterated or undiluted. It was also a misdemeanor to sell or dispose of liquors for gain in any city or town, except for medicinal purposes upon prescription of a regular practicing physician, upon any legal holiday upon which such sale, etc., has been forbidden by a proclamation of the mayor or president of the town board.

IDAHO LIQUOR LAWS, 1887
From the *Annual Report of the Commissioner of Labor*, 1898

Boards of trustees of towns and villages have power to license and regulate dram shops, tippling-houses, and saloons, and to make ordinances and enforce same by fines not exceeding $100 for one offense.

Illegal to keep or erect a booth, tent, stall, etc., for the purpose of selling liquors, for selling such liquors, or for peddling or hawking same within one mile of any camp or field meeting for religious worship during the holding of such meeting.

Misdemeanor to adulterate or dilute any liquor or wine with fraudulent intent to offer, or to cause or permit it to be offered, for sale as unadulterated or undiluted.

Misdemeanor to sell or furnish liquor, or to cause same to be sold or furnished to an Indian.

Later laws were enacted against bringing liquor into or on the premises of a prison, except by direction of prison physician. Selling liquors in any manner, to be drunk on the premises, without a license. Selling or giving intoxicating liquor to any habitual drunkard after receiving notice from a justice of the peace or a judge of probate not to furnish liquors to such drunkard.

Druggists and apothecaries were allowed to sell liquors without license for sacramental purposes or upon prescription of a physician, and may sell alcohol without license for mechanical and scientific purposes.

TEXAS LIQUOR LAWS, 1890S
From the *Annual Report of the Commissioner of Labor*, 1898

The city council of any city shall have power to license, tax, and regulate drinking houses, saloons, barrooms, beer saloons, and all places where liquors are sold; to restrain, regulate, and prohibit the selling or disposing of liquor except by persons duly licensed; to forbid and punish the selling or disposing of liquor to a minor, apprentice, or habitual drunkard; to close on Sunday all places where liquor is sold, and to prescribe the hours such places shall be closed; to prevent the sale or disposing of liquors in any place where theatrical or dramatic representations are given, and to enforce the observance of all rules and ordinances by fines not exceeding $100.

The city councils have power to license every person or firm selling liquor in quantities over a quart, keeping a grog shop, tippling place, barroom, or drinking saloon, or selling liquor in quantities less than one quart, and every person or firm keeping a brewery, beer shop, or distillery. Fine of $10 for each day business is carried on without a license, when license is required.

Licensee can only sell at the place designated in the license. Misdemeanor, punishable as if selling without a license, to sell liquor to be drunk on the premises without filing the proper bond. The licensee will keep an open, quiet, and orderly house; that he will not furnish or allow liquors to be furnished a person under 21 years of age, to a student or habitual drunkard, or to any person after receiving written notice through a peace officer, wife, mother, daughter, or sister not to sell to such person; that he will not permit persons under 21 years of age to remain about his place of business, nor allow games prohibited by the laws of the State to be played there, nor let any portion of his premises to any person for the purpose of conducting such games; that he will not adulterate liquors or knowingly sell adulterated liquors.

Fines between $50 and $500 for fraudulently adulterating for the purpose of sale liquors with any substance injurious to health, or for selling liquors so adulterated knowing them to be such. Fine not exceeding $500 for manufacturing, offering for sale, or selling liquors known to be so adulterated.

WYOMING LIQUOR LAWS, 1880s
REVISED STATUTES OF 1887 from the *Twelfth Annual Report of the Commissioner of Labor,* 1898

The council of any town incorporated under the general incorporation law has the power to license, regulate, and forbid the sale of liquors within the town, or within one (1) mile of the outer boundaries thereof. The penalty carried a maximum fine of $100 for any one offense. Anyone knowingly selling any pernicious or adulterated drink or liquors would be fined no more than $200.

A fine not to exceed $500 was the penalty for adulterating or diluting liquors with fraudulent intent to offer them for sale, or to cause or permit them to be offered for sale, as unadulterated or undiluted, and for fraudulently keeping, selling, or offering for sale such liquors as unadulterated or undiluted.

Anyone selling, attempting to sell, or otherwise disposing of liquors within one (1) mile of any place where a congregation or collection of people are assembled together for religious worship carried a maximum fine of $100. The law did not apply to anyone licensed to run a tavern or grocery and selling the liquors in such tavern or grocery. It was a misdemeanor for any licensee to sell or dispose of liquors between ten (10) o'clock a.m. and two (2) o'clock p.m. on Sunday in towns having a population of five hundred (500) or more, or to sell or dispose of liquors during the day an election is being held between sunup and sunset.

Anyone who shall sell, bring, or convey liquor into any jail for the use of any person confined therein, unless same shall be certified to be necessary for the health of such prisoner by some reputable physician, who shall specify the quantity and quality to be furnished, etc., and on any sheriff, keeper, officer, or other person employed in such jail for permitting liquor to be so sold or used could be fined between $50 and $500.

Anyone deemed a retail dealer could sell or dispose of liquors in quantities less than five (5) gallons or by the case within five (5) miles of any railroad or within five (5) miles of a town, city or village located on any railroad. An annual county license fee of $300 and a special license permit was required. In other cases, the annual fee for a retail dealer is $100. A fine of $150, of which one-half goes to the informer and one-half to county treasury, for selling at retail without a license. Anyone selling liquors by the barrel, case, or in the original package are deemed wholesale dealers, and must each pay an annual county license of $175. A person dealing both by retail and wholesale must take out both kinds of licenses. All fines to be paid into the county treasuries. A maximum fine of $1,000 for anyone selling or disposing of liquors without having first obtained a license, counting, to anyone under twenty-one and then later sixteen, and to a known drunkard.

ENDNOTES

Chapter One

1. http://lewisandclarkjournals.unl.edu/read/?_xmlsrc=1804-06-29&_xslsrc=LCstyles.xsl, June 29, 1804.
2. https://www.monticello.org/site/jefferson/jeffersons-long-look-west, July 3, 1803.
3. http://loc.gov/exhibits/jefferson/168.html.
4. Hiram Martin Chittenden, *The American Fur Trade of the Far West* (New York: Francis P. Harper, 1902).
5. *Donald Jackson, ed., Letters of the Lewis and Clark Expedition: with Related Documents 1783–1854* (Urbana and Chicago: University of Illinois Press, 1978), 69–74
6. https://lewisandclarkjournals.unl.edu/item/lc.jrn.1803-12-25#lc.jrn.1803-12-25.01.
7. https://lewisandclarkjournals.unl.edu/item/lc.jrn.1804-02-20#lc.jrn.1804-02-20.01.
8. http://lewisandclarkjournals.unl.edu/search.php?searchField=whiskey, various dates.
9. http://lewisandclarkjournals.unl.edu/read/?_xmlsrc=1804-02-20&_xslsrc=LCstyles.xsl, February 20, 1804.
10. http://lewisandclarkjournals.unl.edu/read/?_xmlsrc=1804-11-13&_xslsrc=LCstyles.xsl, November 13, 1804.
11. https://lewisandclarkjournals.unl.edu/item/lc.jrn.1805-07-04#lc.jrn.1805-07-04.03.
12. http://lewisandclarkjournals.unl.edu/read/?_xmlsrc=1806-09-06&_xslsrc=LCstyles.xsl, September 6, 1806; http://lewisandclarkjournals.unl.edu/read/?_xmlsrc=1806-09-17&_xslsrc=LCstyles.xsl#noten40091703, September 17, 1806.
13. M. G. Humphreys, *The Boy's Story of Zebulon M. Pike* (New York: Charles Scribner's Sons, 1911).
14. http://user.xmission.com/~drudy/mtman/html/james/jamesint.html.
15. http://user.xmission.com/~drudy/mtman/html/beckwourth/index.html.

16. David Burnet, *Texas in 1840 or, The Emigrant's Guide to the New Republic* (New York: William W. Allen, 1840).
17. Charles Larpenteur, *Forty Years a Fur Trader on the Upper Missouri*, Elliott Coues, ed. (New York: Francis P. Harper, 1898), http://user.xmission.com/~drudy/mtman/html/larpenteur/index.html; Fletcher W. Hewes and Henry Gannett, *Scribner's Statistical Atlas of the United States* (New York: Charles Scribner's Sons, 1883).
18. http://user.xmission.com/~drudy/mtman/html/beckwourth/index.html #ch18.
19. http://user.xmission.com/~drudy/mtman/html/beckwourth/index.html #ch18.

Chapter Two
1. Michael R. Veach, *Kentucky Bourbon Whiskey: An American Heritage* (Lexington: University Press of Kentucky, 2013).
2. David Ames Wells, *Reports of a Commission Appointed for a Revision of the Revenue System of the United States 1865-'66* (US Revenue Commission, 1866).
3. Ibid.
4. *Santa Fe Daily New Mexican*, December 10, 1877.
5. *Denver Post*, December 4, 1902.
6. *Bismarck Tribune*, July 2, 1880.
7. *Times-Picayune* (New Orleans, LA), August 2, 1881.
8. Joseph Fleischman, *The Art of Blending and Compounding Liquors and Wines* (New York: Dick & Fitzgerald, 1885).
9. Interview with David Perkins, distiller at High West Distillery, Park City, Utah, August 2016.
10. *Norfolk Virginian*, May 27, 1897.

Chapter Three
1. *Annals of Wyoming* (Wyoming State Archives and Historical Department, 1970).
2. http://thedigitalvoice.com/enigma/hyd1857b.htm.
3. Ibid.
4. The Americana Society, *American Historical Magazine*, New York, 1908.
5. Josiah Gibbs, *Lights and Shadows of Mormonism* (Salt Lake City: Salt Lake Tribune Publishing, 1909).
6. *Annals of Wyoming*.
7. Frank A. Root and William Elsey Connelley, *The Overland Stage to California* (Crane & Company, 1901).
8. Richard F. Burton, *The City of the Saints* (New York, Harper & Brothers Publishing, 1862).

9. Root and Connelley, *The Overland Stage to California.*
10. Burton, *The City of the Saints* (New York, Harper & Brothers Publishing, 1862).
11. Peter Olsen Hansen, "Journal" (Latter-day Saints, Salt Lake City, ca. 1876), https://history.lds.org/overlandtravel/sources/5078/hansen-peter -olsen-journal-ca-1876-75-77.
12. William Audley Maxwell, *Crossing the Plains Days Of '57* (San Francisco: Sunset Publishing House, 1915).
13. Orson Hyde Elliott, *Reminiscences in the Life of Orson Hyde Elliott* (Salt Lake City: Latter-day Saints, 1899), https://history.lds.org/overlandtravel/ sources/87829/elliott-orson-hyde-reminiscences-in-the-life-of-orson-hyde -elliott-1899-210-216.
14. Barnes, Demas. *From the Atlantic to the Pacific, Overland Via the Overland Stage, 1865, A Series of Letters,* http://www.over-land.com/diarybarnes.html.
15. Root and Connelley, *The Overland Stage to California.*
16. Ibid.
17. Tom Stevens invoice. University of Wisconsin-La Crosse, Murphy Library, Special Collections.
18. *Frank Leslie's Illustrated Newspaper,* January 22, 1876.
19. John McDonald, *Secrets of the Great Whiskey Ring* (Chicago: Belford, Clarke & Co, 1880).
20. Ibid.
21. Ibid.
22. Ibid.
23. John Alexander Joyce, *A Checkered Life* (Chicago: S. P. Rounds, Jr., 1883).
24. *The Herald* (Dallas, TX), August 12, 1885.
25. Mark Twain, *Life on the Mississippi* (Boston: John R. Osgood & Co. 1883).

Chapter Four

1. *San Francisco Chronicle,* May 22, 1896.
2. *Buckhorn Exchange saloon, Denver, Colorado.*
3. *Hermann Advertiser* (Hermann, MO), July 7, 1876.
4. *San Francisco Chronicle,* January 10, 1911
5. *Coffeyville Weekly Journal* (Coffeyville, KS), September 12, 1885.
6. *Daily Tribune* (Lawrence, KS), September 13, 1867.
7. *Topeka Daily Capital,* February 16, 1884.
8. Dr. A. W. Chase, *Dr. Chase's Recipes; or Information for Everybody* (Ann Arbor, MI: R.A. Beal, 1870).
9. *South and West* (Austin, TX), December 19, 1865.
10. *Girard Press* (Girard, KS), May 29, 1879.
11. *Topeka Daily Capital,* December 11, 1885.
12. *The Times* (Clay Center, KS), April 21, 1887.
13. *Garrett Clipper* (Garrett, IN), January 7, 1932.

14. *Helena Herald* (Helena, MT), February 12, 1875.
15. *Independent Record* (Helena, MT), September 7, 1889.
16. "Effects of Intoxication," *Tombstone Daily Nugget* (Tombstone, AZ), September 8, 1881.
17. *Fort Scott Weekly Monitor* (Fort Scott, KS), May 27, 1886.
18. *Fort Scott Weekly Monitor* (Fort Scott, KS), May 20, 1886.
19. *Grand Forks Daily Herald* (Grand Forks, ND), October 7, 1889.
20. *Pacific Wine and Spirit Review* (San Francisco, CA), April 5, 1892.
21. *Leavenworth Weekly Times*, December 16, 1897.
22. *Indianapolis Journal*, January 22, 1896.
23. *Leavenworth Weekly Times*, December 16, 1897.
24. *Argus Leader* (Sioux Falls, SD), February 5, 1896.
25. *Kansas City Star*, September 29, 1906.
26. *Barton County Democrat* (Great Bend, KS), June 13, 1889.
27. Sir Henry Veel Huntley, *California: Its Gold and Its Inhabitants*, in *California as I Saw It* (Library of Congress, WPA).
28. *Anaconda Standard* (Anaconda, MT), February 3, 1899.
29. *Idaho Daily Statesman* (Boise, ID), September 29, 1905.
30. *Salt Lake Telegram*, December 29, 1905.

Chapter Five

1. Zephryin Engelhardt, *The Missions and Missionaries of California* (San Francisco: The James H. Barry Company, 1908).
2. Hubert Howe Bancroft, *The Works of Hubert Howe Bancroft* (San Francisco: The History Company, 1888).
3. John Sutter, http://www.sfmuseum.net/hist2/gold.html.
4. Hubert Howe Bancroft, *The Works of Hubert Howe Bancroft* (San Francisco: The History Company, 1888).
5. Bancroft, *The Works of Hubert Howe Bancroft*.
6. *Evening Bulletin* (San Francisco, CA), August 18, 1877.
7. William Lewis Manly, *Death Valley in '49*, in *California as I Saw It* (Library of Congress, WPA).
8. Heinrich Lienhard, *A Pioneer at Sutter's Fort: The Adventures of Heinrich Lienhard*, in *California as I Saw It* (Library of Congress, WPA).
9. Charles Collins, *Mercantile Guide and Directory for Virginia City, Gold Hill, Silver City and American City, 1864–65* (San Francisco: Agnew & Deffebach, 1864).
10. *Semi-Weekly Wisconsin* (Milwaukee, WI), February 20, 1864 (population).
11. *Salt Lake Herald*, December 25, 1889.
12. *Oregonian* (Portland, OR), June 28, 1861.
13. *Oregonian* (Portland, OR), June 22, 1861.
14. *Oregonian* (Portland, OR), June 24, 1861.
15. *Oregon Statesman* (Salem, OR), August 17, 1863.

ENDNOTES

16. *Dillon Examiner* (Dillon, MT), December 16, 1903.
17. *Montana Post* (Virginia City, MT), February 9, 1867.
18. *Overland monthly and Out West magazine.* Title: "Up in the Po-Go-Nip."
    March 1869; pp. 273-279.
19. *Steamer Alta California* (San Francisco, CA), February 13, 1869.
20. Park City Museum, Park City, UT.
21. *Black Hills Daily Times* (Deadwood, SD), July 15, 1883.
22. Library of Congress, Manuscript Division, WPA Federal Writers' Project
    Collection.
23. *Daily Commonwealth* (Ellsworth, KS), July 1, 1873.
24. Robert Marr White, *Dodge City: The Cowboy Capital* (Wichita, KS: Wich-
    ita Eagle Press, 1913).
25. R. L. Polk, *Polk's Kansas State Gazetteer and Business Directory* (Detroit, 1878).
26. R. L. Polk, *Polk's Kansas State Gazetteer and Business Directory* (Detroit, 1880).
27. George W. Romspert, *The Western Echo* (Dayton, OH: United Brethren
    Publishing House, 1881).
28. *Weekly Commonwealth* (Topeka, KS), June 9, 1881.
29. *McKenney's Business Directory* (L. M. McKenney & Co., 1883).
30. Tom J. Snow, Library of Congress, Manuscript Division, WPA Federal
    Writers' Project Collection.
31. Andre Jorgenson Anderson, Library of Congress, Manuscript Division,
    WPA Federal Writers' Project Collection.
32. Ibid.
33. *Dallas Morning News*, December 11, 1887.
34. Ibid.
35. *Gazette* (Fort Worth, TX), February 26, 1887.
36. *Weekly Times Herald* (Dallas, TX), April 12, 1890.
37. *Weekly Times Herald* (Dallas, TX), June 21, 1890.
38. Bud Brown, Library of Congress, Manuscript Division, WPA Federal
    Writers' Project Collection.
39. Richard Murphy, Library of Congress, Manuscript Division, WPA Federal
    Writers' Project Collection.
40. *Park Record* (Park City, UT), September 1, 1883.
41. *Park Record* (Park City, UT), July 21, 1883.
42. *Park Record* (Park City, UT), October 14, 1882.
43. *Helena Daily Herald* (Helena, MT), October 5, 1876.
44. *Wyandotte Gazette* (Kansas City, KS), March 17, 1876.
45. *Rocky Mountain Husbandman* (Diamond City, MT), June 29, 1876.
46. *Black Hills Daily Times* (Deadwood, SD), June 6, 1877.
47. *Daily News* (Denver, CO), June 23, 1890.
48. *Idaho Daily Statesman* (Boise, ID), October 13, 1888.
49. *Black Hills Daily Times* (Deadwood, SD), November 29, 1878.
50. *Des Moines Register*, March 5, 1879.

51. *St. Joseph Weekly Gazette* (St. Joseph, MO), April 24, 1879.
52. Oscar Wilde, *Impressions of America* (Sunderland: Keystone Press, 1906).
53. Earl Chafin, ed., *Tombstone Letters of Clara Brown* (Earl Chafin Press, 1988).
54. *Tombstone Epitaph* (Tombstone, AZ), June 23, 1881.
55. *Tombstone Republican* (Tombstone, AZ), February 23, 1883; reprint.
56. Cy Warman, *The Prospector: Story of the Life of Nicholas C. Creede* (Denver: The Great Divide Publishing Company, 1894).
57. *Wichita Eagle*, March 23, 1892.
58. Cy Warman, *The Prospector: Story of the Life of Nicholas C. Creede.*
59. *Tombstone Prospector* (Tombstone, AZ), March 8, 1892.
60. *Anderson Intelligencer* (Anderson Court House, SC), March 24, 1892.
61. *St. Paul Daily Globe*, May 22, 1892.
62. *San Francisco Chronicle*, June 6, 1892.
63. *The Wichita Daily Eagle, March 7, 1896.*
64. Colorado Midland Railway Co., *The Cripple Creek Gold Fields, Placers, Lodes*, 1892.
65. *Emporia Gazette* (Emporia, KS), July 27, 1896.
66. Atchison, Topeka and Santa Fe Railway Company, *Cripple Creek* (Passenger Department, 1896).
67. *St. Louis Dispatch*, September 8, 1895.
68. *LA Times*, September 6, 1896.
69. *Rocky Mountain News* (Denver, CO), November 14, 1895.
70. H. H. Paramore, *The Practical Guide to America's New El Dorado: Klondike Gold Fields* (St. Louis: Samuel Myerson Printing Co., 1897).
71. *Beeville Bee* (Beeville, TX), November 19, 1897.
72. *Argus and Patriot* (Montpelier, VT), December 15, 1897.
73. *San Francisco Chronicle*, October 31, 1898.
74. *San Francisco Chronicle*, June 24, 1899.
75. *River Press* (Fort Benton, MT), September 13, 1899.
76. *Duluth News Tribune*, November 15, 1899
77. *San Francisco Chronicle*, November 13, 1899.
78. Lanier McKee, *The Land of Nome: A Narrative Sketch of the Rush to Our Bering Sea Gold-Fields* (New York: Grafton Press, 1902).
79. LaBelle Brooks-Vincent, *The Scarlet Life of Dawson and the Roseate Dawn of Nome*, 1900; https://archive.org/stream/cihm_17990#page/n5/mode/2up/search/whiskey.

Chapter Six

1. I. Mac D. DeMuth, *The History of Pettis County, Missouri* (Lenox and Tilden Foundations, 1896).
2. Major General Grenville M. Dodge, *How We Built the Union Pacific Railway* (Washington, DC: Government Printing Office, 1910).

3. *Detroit Free Press*, September 25, 1883.
4. Samuel Bowles, Library of Congress, Manuscript Division, WPA Federal Writers' Project Collection.
5. Major General Grenville M. Dodge, *How We Built the Union Pacific Railway*.
6. *Semi-Weekly Telegraph* (Salt Lake City, UT), August 16, 1866.
7. *Frontier Index* (Julesburg, CO), July 5, 1867.
8. *Edgefield Advertiser* (Edgefield, SC), July 15, 1868.
9. *San Francisco Bulletin*, June 21, 1867.
10. *Cheyenne Leader* (Cheyenne, WY), July 8, 1868; *Sacramento Union*, July 22, 1868.
11. *Frontier Index* (Laramie, WY), June 23, 1868.
12. *Commercial Record* (Cheyenne, WY), April 11, 1868.
13. *Frontier Index* (Laramie, WY), June 19, 1868.
14. *Frontier Index* (Laramie, WY), May 05, 1868.
15. *Edgefield Advertiser* (Edgefield, SC), July 15, 1868.
16. Samuel Bowles, Library of Congress, Manuscript Division, WPA Federal Writers' Project Collection.
17. *Weston Democrat* (Weston, WV), January 18, 1869.
18. *Frontier Index* (Laramie, WY), October 30, 1868; *Oregonian* (Portland, OR), November 19, 1868.
19. Mrs. Mary Mathews Tolman, Library of Congress, Manuscript Division, WPA Federal Writers' Project Collection.
20. Josiah F. Gibbs, *Lights and Shadows of Mormonism* (Salt Lake City: Salt Lake Tribune Publishing, 1909).
21. *San Francisco Bulletin*, February 27, 1873.
22. *Sacramento Daily Union*, July 7, 1869.
23. Charles H. Walbourn, *Confessions of a Pullman Conductor*, 1913. Original from University of Illinois at Urbana-Champaign.
24. Herbert O. Holderness, *The Reminiscences of a Pullman Conductor* (Chicago, 1901).
25. Oscar Wilde, *Impressions of America* (Sunderland: Keystone Press, 1906).
26. Montgomery Ward, catalog no. 13, spring and summer, 1875.
27. H. T. Wilson, *Historical Sketch of Las Vegas, New Mexico* (Chicago: The Hotel World Publishing Co.).
28. *Las Vegas Gazette* (Las Vegas, NM), October 13, 1880, March 27, 1881.
29. *Daily National Republican* (Washington, DC), April 13, 1871.
30. Fletcher W. Hewes and Henry Gannett, *Scribner's Statistical Atlas of the United States* (New York: Charles Scribner's Sons, 1883).
31. Mark Wymond, *Railroad Valuation and Rates* (Chicago: Wymond & Clark), 1916.
32. *Deadwood Daily Pioneer*, August 20, 1889.
33. *Pacific Wine and Spirit Review* (San Francisco, CA), April 5, 1892.
34. Ibid.

Chapter Seven

1. Distilled Spirits Council of the United States, economics.
2. TTB Distilled Spirits Producers and Bottlers by state, https://www.ttb.gov/foia/xls/frl-spirits-producers-and-bottlers.htm; American Distilling Institute; Statistical Abstract of the United States: 1895 Eighteenth Number, Census Library, 1896.
3. Ian Buxton and Paul S. Hughes, *The Science and Commerce of Whisky* (Cambridge: RSC Publishing, 2014).
4. Wayne Curtis, "The New Science of Old Whiskey," *Atlantic* magazine, November 2013.

Index

Warman, Cyrus, 147
Washington
  Tacoma, 156, 157
Watkins, George, 131, 132
Webster, H., 27
Weibush, Charles, 134
Wells, David, 26
Whealan, Will, 190
Whiskey Ring, 61
White Elephant saloon, 129
Who Would A' Thought It Dance
  Hall, 174
Wilde, Oscar, 139, 183
Wilkinson, James, 9
Williams, Kid, 153
Williams, Yank, 115
Willoughby, Charley, 142
Wilson, H. T., 185
Wimmer, Robert, 52
Women's Christian Temperance
  Union, 95, 96, 97, 101
Wright, Robert M., 125, 128
Wymond, Mark, 188
Wyoming
  Bear River City
    Hell on Wheels, 176
  Benton
    Hell on Wheels, 167, 169, 174,
    175, 176
  Cambria, 190
  Cheyenne, 98, 136, 138, 172
    Hell on Wheels, 167, 169, 170

Evanston
  Hell on Wheels, 167, 169
Fort Bridger, 16, 50, 177
Fort Sanders, 172
Green River, 174
  Hell on Wheels, 167, 169, 170,
  174
Laramie, 172, 173
  Hell on Wheels, 167, 169, 174
Newcastle, 190
Sidney
  Hell on Wheels, 169
Tubtown, 190

Yellowstone Expedition, 4
Young, Brigham, 25, 39, 43, 44, 46,
  48, 56, 103, 119
Yukon Territory, 154, 157, 161
  Bennett City, 158
  Birch Creek mining district, 155
  Circle City, 154, 155, 157
  Dawson, 156, 158, 159
  Discovery Claim, 158
  E. O. Lindblom Placer Claim,
  158
  Eagle City, 145, 157
  Fort Yukon, 157
  No. 1 on Snow Creek Placer
  Claim, 158
  Rampart, 157
  St. Michael, 157
  Weare, 157

About the Authors

Sherry Monahan has been writing nonfiction books and articles about the American West since 1998. She has become the go-to person for food, drink, and daily life details regarding frontier life.

Some of her books include *The Cowboy's Cookbook, Frontier Fare: Recipes & Lore from the Old West, Mrs. Earp: Wives and Lovers of the Earp Brothers, California Vines, Wines, and Pioneers, The Wicked West,* and *Tombstone's Treasures: Silver Mines and Golden Saloons.* Her *Cowboy Cookbook* was awarded a gold Will Rogers Medallion.

She is the past president of Western Writers of America (2014–2016) and has penned a monthly food column for *True West* magazine since 2009. Her stories have also appeared in *Cowboys and Indians, Wild West* magazine, *Arizona Highways,* and other regional publications. Sherry has appeared in numerous History Channel, Fox News, and American Heroes Channel documentaries. In 2010 she was honored with a Wrangler Award for her performance in *Cowboys and Outlaws: Wyatt Earp.* She's also a marketing consultant, professional genealogist, and an honorary Dodge City Marshal.

Jane Perkins has lived in Park City, Utah, with her husband, David, since 2004, pursuing their passion of making whiskey and living in the American West.

In 2008 their High West Distillery became the first legal distillery in Utah since the 1870s. In 2009 the High West Distillery and Saloon opened in historic Old Town Park City and became the "world's only ski-in gastro distillery."

Jane has whiskey in her genes; her great-grandfather made the celebrated Duffy's Pure Malt Whiskey in the late 1800s. Both David and Jane share a zeal for the Old West as well. High West Distillery was named Whiskey Advocate Magazine's "Pioneer of the Year" in 2010 and "Distiller of the Year" in 2016.